CU00803001

38151

HATCHMENTS IN BRITAIN

10

The Development and Use of Hatchments
together with
the Hatchments of Ireland and former British Colonies
and Additions and Corrections to Volumes 1-8

Armorial board for Sir William Cordell, d. 1581 at Melford Hall, Suffolk

10

The Development and Use of Hatchments

together with the
Hatchments of Ireland and former British Colonies and
Additions and Corrections to Volumes 1-8

JOHN E. TITTERTON

PHILLIMORE

1994

Published by
PHILLIMORE & CO. LTD.
Shopwyke Manor Barn, Chichester, West Sussex

© John E. Titterton, 1994

ISBN 0 85033 913 8

Printed and bound in Great Britain by
HARTNOLLS LTD.,
Bodmin, Cornwall.

CONTENTS

ILLUSTRATIONS

ACKNOWLEDGEMENTS

The preparation of this, the final volume in the series would not have been possible without the help and contributions of many people. In a period of over 40 years numerous correspondents have sent additional details not only of the hatchments which have been published in earlier volumes but also of references to the use, decoration and making of hatchments in Britain and abroad. This list is too long to mention each person individually.

However, I am pleased to thank particularly the late Mr. T. Brown (Durham), Mr. D. M. Hallowes (Lancashire and Yorkshire), Mr. C. Harrold (Essex), and Mr. J. Pierrepont (Derbyshire) for their continuing advice and contributions. The efforts of Mr. H. Beckwith of Rhode Island and Mrs Marilyn Peterson of Boston, Massachusetts to hunt down and collect together details of the American hatchments are much appreciated. The Count of Clandermond has provided the same valuable service for Irish hatchments. I am grateful to Mr. R. Clayton, who has reported several new hatchments in the Home Counties, and Mr. Kay Holmes, who read through the text and advised me on presentation.

Mr. Yorke, Archivist of the College of Arms, and Mr. Julian Litten of the Victoria and Albert Museum have been most helpful and have given me guidance to possible sources. I am grateful to the College of Arms for allowing me to include extracts from their archives and to the Guildhall Library, London, for the same. I am indebted to Mr. C J Burnett, Ross Herald, who has allowed me to extract details from his paper on Scottish funeral heraldry.

Finally this work would not have been completed without the efforts of my wife who compiled a computer database of all the hatchments, and typed and re-typed the text.

JOHN E. TITTERTON

1. *Sir Thomas Aston at the death bed of his wife* by John Souch, 1635-6.
(Copyright Manchester City Art Galleries.)

INTRODUCTION

This volume is the tenth and final volume in the *Hatchments in Britain* series. It concludes the survey of hatchments in the British Isles which was started by Mr. P G Summers, FSA, FHS in 1952. The first nine volumes between them detail the surviving hatchments on a county by county basis. The description of each hatchment gives its heraldic blazon and the identity, where known, of the individual at whose death it was painted.

The purpose of this volume is two fold. Its principal contents are to outline the history of the development and use of the hatchment from the 16th century to the present day. This has concentrated on the practices used in England and Wales with occasional references to Scottish examples. The number of Scottish hatchments is only one per cent of the total and details of Scottish practice are covered adequately elsewhere. (A general outline on Scottish hatchments is provided by Mr. C. J. Burnett, Ross Herald, in the introduction to Scotland in Volume 9. For a detailed account of Scottish funeral heraldry, the reader should consult Mr. Burnett's paper on this subject.[1])

The second purpose of this volume is to give details of additions and corrections to the previously published volumes and to record hatchments which have been found in Ireland and former British colonies.

All known surviving hatchments have been included in these ten volumes but no doubt new discoveries will be made as time passes. For example, this volume includes four hatchments at Beverley Minster (Yorks). One would expect that a church so well known and frequently visited would have been covered in the Yorkshire volume. However, the hatchments were in the ringing tower up a flight of 60 steps and discovered by a campanologist who was, luckily, aware of the hatchment series.

The hatchment developed out of the system of heraldic display as a sign of mourning at medieval funerals. It had two features which came to identify it as a hatchment. Its lozenge shape and the use of black or black and white backgrounds behind the arms. Both the origin of these aspects of its appearance and other features are discussed.

From the Restoration of the monarchy in 1660 until the middle of the 19th century they were common features of English gentry society. So common that they are referred to and appear in the works and illustrations to the books of Thackeray and Dickens. Effectively the practice ceased by 1900 but hatchments of the 20th century do exist.

Collectively hatchments provide a record of development and change in heraldic styles and fashions between the 17th and 19th centuries. Shield shapes, and forms of decoration are similar to those found on bookplates, armorial china and monuments. Hatchments developed systems of marshalling to show more than one marriage and also, of displaying the arms of the individual with those of an Office. Some consideration is given to how such aspects developed and changed.

The opportunity has also been taken to record briefly the history of how the survey itself proceeded.

1 Burnett, C. J., *Funeral Heraldry in Scotland* (with particular reference to Hatchments), The Society of Antiquaries of Scotland, Vol 116, 1986

ABBREVIATIONS

B.E.B.	=	Burke's *Extinct and Dormant Baronetcies*
B.E.P.	=	Burke's *Extinct and Dormant Peerages*
B.L.G.	=	Burke's *Landed Gentry*
B.P.	=	Burke's *Peerage, Baronetage and Knightage*
D.N.B.	=	*Dictionary of National Biography*
G.E.C.	=	*The Complete Peerage*, G. E. Cockayne
G.M.	=	*Gentleman's Magazine*
I.G.I.	=	Mormon International Genealogical Index
M.G. & H.	=	*Miscellanea Genealogica et Heraldica*
M.I.	=	Monumental Inscription
M.O.	=	*Musgrave's Obituary*
P.R.	=	Parish Register
V.C.H.	=	*Victoria County History*

1. MARRIED MAN

2. MARRIED WOMAN

3. BACHELOR

4. WIDOW

5. WIDOWER

6. SPINSTER

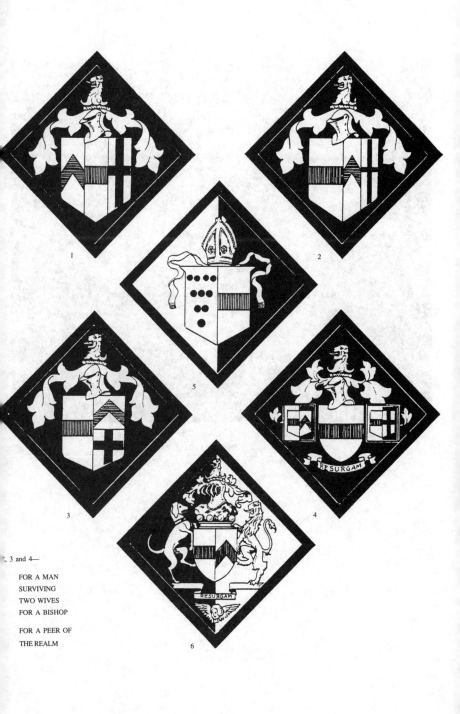

1, 2, 3 and 4—

FOR A MAN
SURVIVING
TWO WIVES

FOR A BISHOP

FOR A PEER OF
THE REALM

2. Hatchment of Sir John Harpur Crewe, 9th Bt. d. 1886 hanging outside Calke Abbey, at the apex of the pediment.
(With permission from the National Trust, Calke Abbey, Derbyshire.)

Chapter 1

Early Background and Development

One problem encountered in tracing the origin and the use of the hatchment is the use of the word 'hatchment' itself. In *An Heraldic Alphabet* by J. P. Brooke-Little (1985), an hatchment is explained as follows: 'The word ... has come to be used exclusively for the achievement of the deceased persons set forth on large diamond-shaped panels'. The definition of achievement is given as: 'a representation of all the armorial devices to which the bearer of arms is entitled. Used in contradistinction to its various parts—arms, crest, supporters, motto, etc'. This distinction between the two words, hatchment and achievement, is quite clear. However, the general acceptance that these are two distinct words each with its own specific meaning probably dates only from the early part of the 19th century. Both words refer to a two-dimensional representation of the shield, crest, helm, etc. which were individual items used by the medieval knight.

From the 16th to the 19th centuries both words (achievement often spelt atchievement) can be found to mean either the general display of a person's armorial devices or the painted diamond-shaped board. It can also refer to the display at funerals of the real three-dimensional items, the crest, shield, helm, surcoat etc. of the deceased. These were carried at the funeral procession and then were erected on the wall of the church after the funeral service. Therefore one must consider critically the context of the word to decide which of the three meanings was intended.

The words hatchment and achievement have a common origin. They can be traced back through documentary sources to the 14th century. The latin version of the word, *hachiamentum*, in 1352 referred to an engraving on a silver plate.[1] An account for work on Royal residences for Henry VI includes 'hachements at the Manor of Sheen'.[2] In 1548 Edward Hall uses 'hachements' to refer to the items carried at the funeral of King Henry V,[3] while Bossewell [4] in 1572 defines the word 'achievement' to be the 'arms of everie gentleman well marshalled with supporters, helme, wreath, creste with mantels & y worde'.

Shakespeare uses the word, referring to the funeral items, in *Hamlet*. Laertes, when mourning the death of his father, Polonius, laments; [5]

> His means of death, his obscure funeral
> No trophy sword nor hatchment o'er his bones
> No noble rite nor funeral ostentation
> Cry to be heard.

The origin of this display of funeral achievements is of long standing. Nisbet[6] refers to the practice in ancient Rome of images and trophies being carried at the funeral procession. The earliest surviving examples in England are to be seen above the tomb of Edward, the Black Prince (d.1376), at Canterbury Cathedral, where there are replicas of his shield, surcoat and helmet with crest. These were his 'achievements', erected after his funeral. At St Mary Redcliffe church in Bristol one can see those of Sir William Penn who died in 1670. Some English churches still have a solitary helm hanging high on the wall which has survived from this practice.

Descriptions of funeral processions and services for the 16th and 17th centuries can be found in the records of the College of Arms who were responsible for arranging such events. (Probably this duty arose from the medieval herald's duty of identifying the dead on the battlefield from the heraldic attire of the bodies.) Some of these accounts have been published. 'The Ceremonial for the funeral of William, Lord Grey of Wilton' (d.1562), is printed by the Camden Society, Old Series, No 40. The funeral of Lord Williams of Thame (d.1559) was printed as part of his biography published at Thame in 1873.[7] These two funerals took place only three years apart and the account of the basic procedure is identical. It is worthwhile considering the normal form of these events because the first hatchments survive from 60 years after that date and, as will be shown, develop from the use of heraldry at funerals.

The funeral in its broadest terms may be considered to have three parts. Firstly, there is the preparation of the body and the lying in state at the house of the deceased; secondly, there is the journey or procession from the house to the church; thirdly there is the funeral service and interment in the church. There may be an additional journey involved, if the person died away from home.

Lord Williams died at Ludlow Castle and after his body was 'cold, it was bowelled, trammelled and wrapped in linen' and then placed in a coffin. This was then transported to his house at Rycote, Oxon, in a vehicle 'garnyssed with scotcheons'.

All elements of these two funerals were heraldically decorated. Both coffins were covered with a 'pawle of black velvet' containing 24 yards with eight yards of white satin and decorated with escutcheons of the deceased and his wife. About the corpse were set 'the banner and bannerolls and other hatchments'. The room where the body lay and other rooms in the house were decorated. Lord Grey had died at Cheshunt, the home of his son-in-law, Henry Denny. There, the parlour, where Lord Grey lay in state, and the 'greate chamber were hanged with brode blacke clothe, and the halle, steyres, inner courte tyll without the myddle gate, were hanged with cottons garnished with schoocheons'. The extent of the decoration at the house depended upon the rank of the deceased. (A list of items appropriate to a viscount, baronet and gentleman are reproduced in Appendix 1, No 1.5.).[8]

The church was similarly decorated. For Lords Grey and Williams the interior was covered with cloth. A strong wooden hearse, a free standing structure, was erected in the chancel. It was about 14 ft. long and 9 ft. wide, and had joists above and rails around it. The hearse for Lord Williams was decorated with a large number of heraldic devices. These included: 'eschosseons of metal wrought on buckram, a valence with his motto *a tous venaur*', a Majesty escutcheon under the joists of 'sarcenett lined with buckram wrought in the mydes with his arms and crest and beasts in every corner his badge or crest, a wheel', further arms with supporters on pasteboard and two bannerols, one of his father's arms alone and one of Bladlowe and Starkey quarterly (his first wife's).

There were ten dozen pennoncels (pencils) attached around the hearse. In the centre of the hearse was a table, to receive the coffin, covered with cloth and decorated with escutcheons.

The funeral procession to the church was strictly ordered and again its size depended on the rank of the deceased. The first group were civil and ecclesiastical figures, which included those bearing the standard and the banner. Then came the Officers of Arms carrying the deceased's achievements. At both funerals, Rouge Dragon Pursuivant bore the helm and crest and Chester Herald bore the targe. The coat of arms was carried by Clarenceux, King of Arms for Lord Grey and by Norroy, King of Arms for Lord

Williams. Garter, King of Arms, who was present only at Lord
Grey's funeral, followed Clarenceux and immediately preceded the
body into the church. During the procession there were gentlemen
bearing a bannerol at each corner of the corpse. For Lord Grey
these four displayed one of the following; the impaled arms of
himself and his wife, and of his parents, his grandparents and great
grandparents. The four bannerols of Lord Williams, who could not
claim such a long illustrious pedigree, were for himself, himself
and his first wife, himself and his second wife, and his mother.

After the corpse came the immediate family followed by other
attenders:

> In which order they proceeded to the church, where the corpse placed
> under the hearse, the hatchments thereon, viz. the helmet in the myddst
> with the swerde and target lying on eyther side, the cote hanging on
> theade (i.e. at the head), the morners within the rayles and standerd
> without at the feate the bannerolls holden at the iiij corners.'

As part of the service the hatchments were offered up to God.
The purpose of this was to offer to God the achievements that the
deceased had made in the service of God in his lifetime. After the
service the various officers and mourners returned to the house to
dine, while the body was buried. The hatchments and bannerols
were set up on the church walls in the afternoon on the day of the
funeral for Lord Grey and on the following morning for Lord
Williams. In this context it is clear that the hatchment is the
arrangement of the crest, coat of arms, banners etc.

The hatchments remained with the coffin at all times until
interment took place. They were placed on or around the coffin
while it lay in state at home: then they formed part of the funeral
procession to the church: at the church they were placed on or
around the coffin, then again displayed during the service and
finally after an interval of a few hours placed upon the church
walls where they stayed until they rotted away or were removed at
a Herald's Visitation.

Funerals of the Scottish nobility in the 16th and 17th centuries
followed the same pattern as in England but perhaps with grander
processions. At Lord Hugh Fraser's funeral in 1576, 2,000 men
accompanied his remains to the burial ground.[9] Later when Lord
Lovat died in April 1672 his coffin, accompanied by mourners,
passed through an avenue of three hundred armed clansmen on its
way to the church. After the succession of James VI to the throne

of England, such large gatherings caused concern and two Acts of Parliament were passed through the Scottish Parliament to try to reduce their size.

In England the church was blackened using black baize; in Scotland it seems that part of the church was actually painted black.[10] Scottish practice may be closer to that on the continent where, in France at least, a black band was painted inside the church which was decorated with the arms of the deceased.

In both the funerals of Lord Grey and Lord Williams there is described a 'Majestie' escutcheon. This was hung in the joists so that the deceased was looking up at it. In *The Book of Monuments*, 1619, College of Arms MS. I.1, there is a design for the hearse of Anne of Denmark, Queen of James I. This design shows her facing a diamond-shaped painting of the arms of England impaling Denmark with supporters. Likewise the description of the lying in state of General Monk, Duke of Albemarle, in 1670 by Francis Stafford includes a Majesty escutcheon at the head.[11] The illustration shows a diamond-shaped painting of a coat of arms.[12] There is no indication that the Majesty escutcheon was hung in the church after the funeral. Possibly it was removed when the hearse was dismantled. Some form of two dimensional achievement was erected in churches as early as 1530 because the herald undertaking the Visitation of London that year was charged to 'deface and take away ... any markes or devyces put in Scochyns, Squares or Losenges' which were used against the laws of Honour.[13]

The description of the decoration of the house of Lords Grey and Williams showed that 'the halle, steyres, inner courte tyll without the myddle gate, were hanged with cottons garnished with schoocheons'. These escutcheons were not achievements. The escutcheon was only a shield with no crest or mantling and continued to be used from the 16th century through to the 19th century. The escutcheons used to decorate the hearse and pall seem to have been on silk, buckram or paper. The account of the funeral of Sir Gervase Clifton, in 1666, details the numbers and locations of these devices (see Appendix 1, No. 1.6).[14] His funeral decoration also included a large achievement which was to be placed over the hall porch. Several other references from 1660 are found of hatchments being erected over the gates or doors. The earliest is for 'One Hatchment in Oyle to stand over the gate' which was made for the funeral of Richard de Burgh, Earl of St Albans in 1635 (see Appendix 1, No 1.3).[15]

How far back can this practice be traced? Part of the decoration for the funeral of Sir Thomas Stanley Kt., d. 25 August 1560, included a 'hatchement wrought onto buckram with ye armes helme crest and mantle and supporters with gold and silver'(see Appendix 1, No. 1.1).[16] This is in addition to the helm crest etc. to be put up in the church. Its intended purpose is not stated but one may presume that the hatchment in oil was intended for the house rather than the church. This document may indicate that the practice was not universal at this time because Sir Thomas' funeral is the only one out of a number detailed in this source which includes such an item.

There can be no suggestion at this date of any intention to transfer the hatchment to the church. The achievements were erected there within hours of the funeral service. The hatchment was a painted achievement intended as part of the general heraldic decoration of the residence of the deceased.

1. PRO,E36/278 f.45; Cf. Calendar of the Register of the Black Prince, H.M.S.O. 1930-3, vol. 4, p.72. *The Dictionary of Medieval Latin* from British Sources cites the origin of the word as Old French.
2. PRO E101/503/12.
3. Hall, Chronicles, Henry V, 50.
4. Bossewell, Armorie II, 121b.
5. *Hamlet*, Act 4, Scene 5, 211.
6. Nisbet, A., *A System of Heraldry*, (1722), p.4.
7. These two documents are the source of the subsequent details of these two funerals.
8. See British Library Add Ms 38141 f.8 which gives details for archbishops, dukes, etc. down to the rank of gentleman.
9. Burnett, C. J., *Funeral Heraldry in Scotland*, with particular reference to Hatchments, Society of Antiquaries of Scotland, vol. 116 (1986).
10. Burnett, C. J., *op cit.*
11. Sandford, F., The Order and Ceremonies used for and at the Solemn Interment of ... George Duke of Albemarle ... (London, 1670).
12. This illustration is reproduced in Litten, J., *The English Way of Death* (1991), p.193.
13. Wagner, A. R., *Heralds and Heraldry in the Middle Ages* (1956), p.139. 14 British Library, Add Ms 38141 f.23.
15. College of Arms, Painter's Work Book 12 f.45 16 College of Arms I 13 f. 30. The items for this funeral are detailed in Appendix 1. No. 1.1.

Chapter 2

Hatchments, Armorial Boards and Memorial Boards

The two distinctive features of a hatchment are its diamond-shaped frame (i.e. a square hung from one corner) and the use of either an all black background or partially white/partially black background to the arms.

The earliest positively dated hatchment in Britain is 1629 at Eye in Herefordshire. There are some whose identity is not certain but which could be earlier; in particular, one at St Chad's, Shrewsbury, is probably for Sir Vincent Corbet, Kt., who died 1622/3. Even earlier is that 'probably' for Sir Thomas Vincent, Kt., who died in 1613 at Snowshill Hall, Gloucestershire. There are none which are suggested to be before 1600. There are also two 'square' hatchments at Lydiard Tregoze: one may be dated 1597, the other is for Anne, the first wife of Sir John St John, 1st Bt., who died in 1628. This board has the correct half black, half white background and is one of the earliest instances of its use.

The diamond shape was probably introduced from the Low Countries, and predates British hatchments by 25 years or more. As in Britain the practice has continued to the present century. However, the Dutch hatchments or mourning boards differ from English hatchments in that the partially black and white background was not used[1] and there is further heraldic decoration with shields representing the deceased's antecedents. A similar practice is found on Scottish hatchments.[2]

There is one board which perhaps shows the form from which the hatchment developed. It is now at Melford Hall, Suffolk, and is associated with Sir William Cordell (d.1581).[3] The board is square but has a diamond shape imposed over it. In addition to the central coat of arms, which has four small shields at each corner, there are eight further coats in the border around it (similar to Dutch and Scottish practice). The smaller shields relate to Sir William's wife's family. Lady Cordell died after her husband, but the background to the central area is light and that around the eight shields in the border is black. This may not have been painted for the funeral but

7

as a memorial board. Whatever its purpose it shows a transitional
step to the later conventional hatchment (see frontispiece).

From the latter half of the 16th century heraldically decorated
square or rectangular panels, principally painted on wood, were
put up in churches. The straightforward square heraldic panel
displayed the achievement of the individual. In any documentary
reference these too would be called hatchments.

As well as the square heraldic panel there are both square- and
diamond-shaped heraldic panels which include some form of
inscription. If that inscription is brief and only gives the name and/
or date of death of the individual then the diamond-shaped ones
have been considered as hatchments. Sometimes the identity is
contained in initials or cypher only.

On some examples the inscription is much longer, containing
expressions such as 'near here lies buried' or 'in memory of'. It
is obvious from this that the board never hung above the principal
door of a residence but was hung in the church as a memorial.

Messrs. Bayley and Steer[4] in their article on 'Painted Heraldic
Panels' suggest that many of the square or rectangular heraldic
panels to be seen in churches were the escutcheons which
accompanied the body to the church and were then put up in the
church with a similar purpose to the erection of the achievements
of the nobility. They argue that the diamond-shaped hatchments
had a purpose completely different from that of the square or
rectangular armorial boards. The conclusion of their argument is
that the square board was erected at the church and the diamond-
shaped one at the house. The use of partial white background
appeared on square boards before it did on diamond-shaped ones,
and this may support this argument. The split background was used
on the funeral escutcheons[5] of Viscount Savage (d.1635), but his
hatchment, at Long Melford, has an all black background.[6] His
wife survived him by 15 years. Other early hatchments have an all
black background where clearly the wife has survived.[7]

However, such a division into two functions, based purely on
shape, may be too simple. In addition to the references to Majestie
escutcheons (see Chapter 1), there is other evidence to show that
diamond-shaped panels accompanied the funeral procession. A
painting by Pieter Saenredam (1597-1665) of a *Dutch Church Interior*
shows hatchments displayed on the columns of the church.[8] It also
shows in the background a funeral procession which is led by
someone carrying a diamond-shaped panel. The description of the
funeral of Bishop Juxon at Oxford in 1663 includes a diamond-

shaped achievement. These panels might be identified with the Majesty escutcheons and achievements found in documentary sources. Both square- and diamond-shaped devices were hanging in churches as early as 1530.[9]

During the course of the hatchment survey details have been received of over one hundred heraldically painted panels, many of which can be dated. Consideration of them together with all recorded hatchments dated pre-1700 suggests that one might divide the boards into four categories as follows:

a. Armorial only, i.e. no inscription at all.
b. Inscription limited to name and date of death.
c. Full inscription with phrases such as 'In memory of', 'Near here lies buried' perhaps associated with more than one individual or generation.
d. Other, such as recording a gift to a parish.

These four categories can then be sub-divided by the shape of frame. The following tables show the number in each category divided up by period. There are a number of boards and hatchments, which though clearly 16th or 17th century, are not included because the date is not accurately known. The number of square and rectangular panels will not be a full record of those surviving because the survey was seeking diamond-shaped hatchments; nevertheless, the number is sufficient to give a good indication of the overall pattern.

a. Armorial only, i.e. no inscription at all

Shape	Pre 1601	1601 to 1625	1626 to 1650	1651 to 1675	1676 to 1700	Post 1700
Square/Rect	2	2	0	1	4	12
Diamond	0	2[10]	7	25	41	4600*

b. Inscription limited to name and date of death

Shape	Pre 1601	1601 to 1625	1626 to 1650	1651 to 1675	1676 to 1700	Post 1700
Square/Rect	0	0	4	4	4	1
Diamond	0	0	4	10	10	100*

c. Full inscription, phrases such as 'In memory of' etc.

Shape	Pre 1601	1601 to 1625	1626 to 1650	1651 to 1675	1676 to 1700	Post 1700
Square/Rect	2	3	12	22	18	11
Diamond	0	1	0	2	9	40*

d. Other, such as recording a gift to a parish

Shape	Pre 1601	1601 to 1625	1626 to 1650	1651 to 1675	1676 to 1700	Post 1700
Square/Rect	0	1	1	0	2	12
Diamond	0	0	0	0	0	10*

* Approximate figure.

Table 1. Relative Numbers of 'Armorial' boards by shape, content and date.

The fact that there are both diamond- and square-shaped memorial boards suggests that these two shapes had an element of choice in their use rather than just function. The use of the half black and half white background also occurs on both shaped boards. In each category the impression is given that the square board was used first and then replaced by the diamond-shaped one. The conclusion must be that at this early period the distinction between the diamond-shaped and square-shaped board did not automatically imply one use or the other. At Compton Wynyates, Warwickshire, there are five rectangular-shaped boards for the first five Earls of Northampton (dated 1630 to 1754) and 12 diamond-shaped hatchments for members of the family from 1740 to 1864.

Perhaps the square/rectangular armorial board had a particular purpose which died out; alternatively the use of that shape became unfashionable.[11] The above evidence suggests that it was this specific shape rather than purpose which died out from 1700. The inference is that, prior to this, there was some display at the house and also at the church which could be on either a square- or lozenge-shaped panel.

1. Bayley, Rev. T. D. S. and Steer, Francis W., 'Painted Heraldic Panels', *The Antiquaries Journal*, vol. 35, January-April 1955, p.74. The background was all black for married people and all white for single people.
2. Burnett, C. J., *op cit.*
3. A description of this board is included in Chapter 8, under Suffolk.
4. See footnote 1.
5. College of Arms, Painters Work Book 12.
6. This hatchment is the illustration for Suffolk in Volume 2.
7. I am grateful to Mr. D. M. Hallowes for this analysis.
8. Royal Academy of Arts exhibition of 'Dutch Pictures 1450-1750' in 1952/3, exhibit 527.
9. Wagner, A. R., *op cit.*
10. These are the two 'probable' ones for Sir Vincent Corbet, Kt., d.1622/3 at Old St. Chad's, Shropshire, and Sir Thomas Vincent Kt. (d.1613), at Snowshill Manor, Gloucestershire.
11. See chapter 6 for a more detailed discussion on the background to the diamond shape.

Chapter 3

Hatchments prior to 1700

One can show that a hatchment was hung outside the home, probably from before 1600. (As has been stated previously, the earliest reference traced for a hatchment 'to stand over the gate' is for the Earl of St Albans who died in 1635.) In *The Diary of Thomas Wood*, which is set in Oxford,[1] there are references to hatchments being hung at the gates and entrances of Oxford colleges in the period 1660-1680. One cannot be certain that they were all diamond-shaped. It is also difficult to trace the point which saw the hatchment being transferred to the church after a suitable period of mourning.

Two hatchments for 'the doors' were made at the death of Sir James Drax in March 1661/2. These two hatchments were altered a year later upon the death of his successor, also Sir James.[2] No details are given as to the alterations. As the hatchments do not survive, one cannot tell if it was a simple matter of changing the impaled arms. In old St Chad's, Shrewsbury, there is a hatchment of the Corbet family. The initials, S. V. C. K., suggest it was made for Sir Vincent Corbet Kt., who died in 1622/3. The final quarter is that of his wife, an heiress of the Humfreston family. The initial conclusion is that this was either painted in error or added later as an alteration for another member of the family.[3]

The reference for Sir James Drax shows that it was not uncommon for two hatchments to be painted. Sir William Bucknall, Kt., had two painted for the two fronts of his house.[4] Did Sir James Drax have one house with two fronts or were there two houses? Occasionally the marshalling of the arms is specified and it is clear that the two hatchments need not be the same. Two were painted for Edward, 2nd Viscount Irwine (d.1688); one was 'single with his 4 quarterly coats, ye other impaled with his and her quarterings'.[5]

Surviving examples of this practice can be seen by comparing the two hatchments recorded for Thomas Habington of Hindlip. One is at Spetchley Park (Worcestershire, Vol. 10) and the other is

1 1

at Lower Brockhampton House (Herefordshire, Vol. 9). Even the escutcheons for decorating the house, carriage and church could be different. Sir William Goldbould, who died in 1687,[6] had an achievement with a single coat, but of the 36 escutcheons, 24 were of a single coat, six showed the impaled arms of one wife, and six showed the impaled arms of the other.

Sometimes, when more than one hatchment is painted, there is an indication for their intended destination. Some clients paid for 'setting up the work in London', for others there was a fee either for the man's journey to the country or for a box to carry it in. Some indicate that a hatchment was intended to be erected in a church. The following examples are from Artists' Work Books at the College of Arms.[7]

Date	Detail	Price
c.Sept 1656	Annabella, dau. of William Hamble Esq at Lambeth for a hatchment at the church	£1-10-00
c.Sept 1656	funeral of Lt. Col. Edward Bellamy[8] hatchment for the church	£1-00-00
No date	Justice Thomas Austine of Hodsdon (wife Wilson) buried at Shoreditch 6 Nov.[9] for mending the hatchment	no price
c.Dec1661	Mr. Wilmer's child at Bow for a hatchment to hang in the church	£1-10-00
30 Mar 1688	Porter impaling Chisburne a yard square for the church	no price
5 Apr 1688	Mawgridge impaling Knight a 3/4 board Atch(ievement) for the church[10] at Greenwich	no price

These examples suggest different practices. Those for Lt. Col. Bellamy and Mr Mawgridge were painted for the church at the time of the funeral. Were these used instead of the three -dimensional achievements? Justice Austine's hatchment was repaired. Is this after being damaged by the weather outside his home and before being transferred to the church? It has not been possible to trace the dates of death of Mr. Wilmer's child or of Mr. Porter. They could fall into either category. This limited evidence suggests that some were erected at the church at the time of the funeral and others were repaired before being transferred to the church. (As will be seen in Chapter 4, this confused picture continues in the 18th century.)

The nobility already had their achievements hanging in the church, so in England at least they had no need of the hatchment at the church. In Scotland two hatchments were painted, one for the church and one for the house. The one for the church was hung in conjunction with the achievements of the deceased to form a Cabinet d'Armes.[11] Again Scottish practice is closer allied to that on the continent. A similar result could have been achieved in English churches if the Majesty escutcheon had been hung with the achievements. There is no evidence to suggest this happened.

One further point which can be considered from these entries is the size of early hatchments. Dimensions are occasionally given. Can one assume that the higher the price the larger the hatchment? This should hold true in most cases. Many early hatchments are painted on wood whilst others are on canvas. There is no indication as to whether different charges were made for the same size hatchment but on different materials. Some descriptions and prices are as follows:

Description	Cost
hatchment for church	£1-00-00
hatchment for church	£1-10-00
small hatchment	£2-00-00
a hatchment	£2-10-00
a hatchment	£3-00-00
hatchment one yard square	£3-00-00
great hatchment	£3-00-00
great hatchment	£4-00-00
great hatchment an Ell square	£4-00-00

An ell is equal to one and a quarter yards and this seems to be the largest used at this time. In the 17th and 18th centuries hatchments tended to standardise upon an ell square or a yard and a half square. From the above list one can see that a standard size had not yet developed in the 1650s and 1660s. This is confirmed by the hatchments which have been recorded in the survey. With the occasional exception those smaller than an ell date from the 17th century.

The dating of the surviving hatchments suggests that, at the Restoration, the monarchy's return from exile in the Low Countries, where hatchments were popular, resulted in increased popularity for hatchments in England.[12] There is limited documentary evidence to support this. One of the Painters' Work Books[13] in the College of Arms covers the period 1634 1689. The first two thirds covers the pre-Commonwealth period and lists the heraldry requirements for gentry funerals. There are few if any hatchments. The last third of the book covers the Restoration period and hatchments are a frequent request. However, the user of the book for the first period may have been dealing with a different aspect of the 'funeral market' from the second period.

It has been suggested that the hatchment was developed by the gentry class so that they could have a modest heraldic display at their time of death to echo the grand funerals of the nobility organised by the College of Arms. However it must be remembered that the gentry were allowed to have a display of their own in the church. One further problem is that the accepted view of the true hatchment implies a delay of the period of mourning before transfer to the church, whereas the achievements of the nobility were erected at the church within hours of the funeral service. This idea must be modified. From the evidence discussed earlier, it is clear that hatchments were painted for the church.

Economic factors may well have led to the use of hatchments at both the house and church by the gentry in the early 17th century, instead of a funeral organised by the Heralds. Francis Leveson Esq., who died in 1667, had the full funeral appropriate to his rank. The hatchment for the front of his house cost £3, while the achievements for the wall of the church totalled £8 15s. 6d.[14] Other items used to decorate his house and church cost a further £10 18s. 2d. His funeral was attended by Norroy, King of Arms, and Rouge Dragon, Pursuivant, each of whom charged a fee of £20 and also travelling expenses of £13 each (one shilling per mile). Many of the less well off gentry must have seen advantages in not involving the College of Arms. To use a hatchment instead of the achievements would represent a saving of over £5, but the absence of the Heralds would have saved Francis Leveson £66.[15]

Although peers had hatchments painted for the house, as with the Earl of St Albans above, very few have survived from the 17th century. They represent only five per cent of the hatchments for that period, including their spouses. They are:

Thomas, 1st Viscount Savage (d.1635), at Long Melford, Suffolk.
Josceline, 11th Earl of Northumberland (d.1670), at Tadcaster, Yorkshire.
Mary, wife of William, 3rd Viscount Saye and Sele (d.1676), at Broughton, Oxon.
Leicester, 6th Viscount Hereford (d.1677), at Sudbourne, Suffolk.
Sophia, wife of Edward, 1st Viscount Wimbledon (d.1691), Kedington, Suffolk.
Mary, wife of Charles, 6th Earl of Dorset (d.1691), at East Grinstead, Sussex.

A wife or widow could not display the military achievements of her husband. One can compare the heraldic items made for the funerals of Elizabeth Countess of Rochester in 1687 and Lord Coventry in 1689.[16] (The similarity of these items to those used at funerals both a hundred years earlier and a hundred years later is striking.)[17] Most items are common but Lord Coventry had a 'Majestie' escutcheon and his achievements. So for the ladies of the nobility and for the wives of the gentry the transfer of the painted hatchment from the house to the church may have seemed the only way of having a lasting display at the church. For the gentry the use of a hatchment was the more economic way.

This early period of use of hatchments by the gentry occurred as the control of the College of Arms over funerals was waning. The financial motivation is suggested above. That the hatchments of the nobility first survive in any numbers in the 18th century, when the College of Arms no longer controlled funerals, would tend to support this suggestion.

However, there was another activity of the College of Arms which ceased at this time and this may have greater influence on the numbers of surviving hatchments. During the 16th and first half of the 17th centuries the Heralds conducted their 'Visitations' county by county. Most counties received three or four and a few were visited five or six times.

In the Visitation of London 1530[18] the herald defaced and took away escutcheons, squares and lozenges. If this act was repeated in the shires during the Visitations over the next hundred years then a number of hatchments for the gentry will have been lost. This activity by the Heralds cannot be ignored when considering the survival of hatchments.

The conclusion must be that hatchments emerged in the 16th century within the heraldic display at the deceased's home (or homes) as part of the funeral activities of the nobility. This practice increased in the 17th century. Hatchments were hung above the doors or gate of the deceased's residences. Originally this form may not have been diamond-shaped but the diamond shape will have been more practical. In the 17th century the gentry seem to have taken to displaying them in churches as well as outside their homes. By about 1700 the diamond-shaped hatchment had replaced the square and rectangular panels. Some were erected at the church whilst others were transferred to the church from the house after repair if necessary. By around 1725 they were accepted as part of the normal procedure and used by the nobility and gentry alike.

1.   Clark, A., (ed.), *The Life and Times of Anthony Wood*, Oxford Historical Society, vols. 19, 21, 26, 30, 40.
2.   College of Arms, IB 7 pp.79 and 94.
3.   See also section on marshalling in Chapter 6. This may not be an error.
4.   British Library, Add Ms 26683 f.50.
5.   College of Arms, IB 14 p.161.
6.   College of Arms, IB 14 p.12.
7.   College of Arms, IB 7, which covers the period 1656-64 and IB 14 which covers the period 1687-9.
8.   Edward Bellamy was buried 4 September 1656 (Lambeth Parish Register).
9.   This is 1658, (Shoreditch Parish Register).
10. Mr. Mawgridge was buried 9 April 1688 (Greenwich Parish Register).
11. See Burnett, C. J., *op cit.*, Illustration 8.
12. Table 2 in Chapter 4 details the number of surviving hatchments for 20-year intervals.
13. College of Arms, Painters' Work Book 2, 1634-89.
14. British Library, Add Ms 38141, f.28. See Appendix 1, 1.7 for full transcript.
15. See Raines, Rev. F. R. (ed.), Letters on the Claims of the College of Arms in Lancashire in the Time of *James I*, Chetham Society, Vol. 96, 187. These letters outline the gentry's efforts to evade the necessary fees.
16. See Appendix 1, 1.8.
17. See the various documents in Appendix 1.
18. Wagner, A. R., *op cit.*

Chapter 4

Hatchments in the 18th and early 19th Centuries

The popularity of hatchments increased throughout the 18th century and continued until the accession of Queen Victoria. Table 2 shows the numbers of surviving hatchments, which can be dated, summated for 20-year periods. It is reasonable to assume that the earlier a hatchment was painted then the less will be the chance of its survival to the present day. One should therefore increase the figures for the 17th and early 18th centuries to obtain a more accurate profile of their popularity.

Period	No. Recorded
up to 1640	11
1641-1660	29
1661-1680	30
1681-1700	48
1701-1720	110
1721-1740	167
1741-1760	200
1761-1780	288
1781-1800	400
1801-1820	603
1821-1840	881
1841-1860	728
1861-1880	436
1881-1900	119
Post 1900	111

Table 2. Numbers of surviving hatchments by period

The most popular period was the 1830s, with Queen Victoria's year of accession in 1837 having the highest individual figure of seventy-two. Whilst hatchments do age and deteriorate, resulting in eventual loss, the principal causes of destruction will affect hatchments of all ages. Fire, leaking church roofs or church restoration will affect all hatchments in the church, not only the oldest. It will be shown later that perhaps only one in twenty of all hatchments painted have survived. The heraldic displays associated with funerals changed very little from 1550 to 1800. This can be demonstrated by comparing the heraldic items required for funerals over this period for the nobility, the gentry and their ladies, some examples of which are given in Appendix 1. For all classes the display of heraldry remained an important part of the funeral process, both at the house, on the journey to the service, and at the church. The funerals of the nobility were the grander affairs but the gentry used parallel if more modest displays.

The main change over the period was that the required heraldic items were no longer regulated or provided by the College of Arms. The commissioning, production and erection of a hatchment was just one item amongst many required for the funeral. The funeral was organised by an executor of the deceased who could either co-ordinate the various aspects himself or engage an undertaker.

The herald painter was only one of the tradesmen that the executor or undertaker would approach to bring together the final result. Many London undertakers had premises around St Paul's churchyard.

3. Trade card of W. Barton of 20 St Saviour's churchyard, Borough (London). *Bodleian Library, John Johnson Collection, Trade cards Vol. XXVIII.)*

For many, undertaking was only one aspect of their employment. Some were employed in aspects of the wood-working trade, probably because of the need for coffins. Others were upholsterers, linen drapers, or even auctioneers.[1]

Richard Carpenter was an undertaker in London operating in the 1740s. The Guildhall Library has details of his accounts for 1746-1747.[2] One of his 'customers' was the Earl of Darnley who died 22 July 1747 and was buried the following 1 August at Westminster Abbey. The heraldic items were produced by a Mr. Ware and included two achievements and many of the items associated with a grand Tudor funeral (see Appendix 1, 1.10). The wooden coffin and case was produced by a Mr. Gladman, a lead coffin by a Mr. Goodwin, the coffin plate by a Mr. Nowell, which was then engraved by a Mr. James Wigley. A Mr. John Lodmyton provided 25 white plumes. These same tradesmen were employed by Mr. Carpenter for other, more modest funerals. The hatchment for Mrs. Elizabeth Monoux (No. 6, at Wootton, Bedfordshire), was produced by Mr. Ware for Mr. Carpenter.

One of these tradesmen, James Wigley, may have been employed by the executor of Capt. John Stevens of Badgemore House, Berkshire, some thirty years later. The funeral arrangements of this gentleman may be typical of the events for minor county gentry where an undertaker was not engaged.

Capt. John Stevens died at his home, Badgemore House, Wargrave, Berkshire, at 4.20 p.m. on Monday 28 April 1777.[3] His executor contacted a local carpenter, Mr. Walter Powney, to make a (wooden) coffin. Mr. John Wheeler, a local plumber, was asked to produce a lead coffin 'with inscription on its breast'. On Tuesday evening a letter was written to Mr. Bigland to order Mr. Sarney to provide a hatchment and Mr. James Wigley to engrave a plate. Both these latter gentlemen operated from London.

Mr. Bigland may well be identified with Garter Bigland. Mr. Wigley must have been connected with Mr. James Wigley, the engraver employed by Mr. Carpenter in 1747 and referred to above. The coffin plate arrived from London on Saturday 3 May. The funeral took place at Wargrave church on Friday 9 May 1777. Mr. Josiah Sarney produced the hatchment on 8 May but it does not seem to have been erected until the day after the funeral, i.e., on 10 May. This was done by Mr. Walter Powney, who had made the coffin, together with Mr. Richard Powney. The executors were charged four shillings for two men for one day for doing this.[4]

4. Hatchment of
John, 3rd Duke of
Rutland, KG,
d. 1779, at Bottesford
church, Leicester,
and painted by the
workshop of Thomas
Sharpe of London.
(*Photograph by
J. E. Titterton.*)

The herald painter would work for either the executor or the undertaker engaged by the executor. An undertaker is more likely to be engaged for the larger funerals. Appendix 1, Nos. 1.11, 1.12, and 1.13 show the number of items required for Lady Petre (d.1787), Mrs. Gale (d.1791), and Lord Petre (d.1801). These were produced by the workshop of Thomas Sharpe.[5] Lord and Lady Petre's were produced for the 'undertaker'. Mrs. Gale's were produced for her executors.

Thomas Sharpe and his successor, George Bishop, were established at St Benet's near the College of Arms. Although based in London, Thomas Sharpe worked for families who lived, and died, outside London such as Mrs. Gale and Lord and Lady Petre. Work for some families in the shires was probably gained through his association with the College of Arms or because the family had a town house in addition to a country house. As well as from London, orders were received from clients operating in Bath, Bromley, Chelmsford, Chichester, Coventry, Croydon, Kingston, Luton, Northampton, Norwich, Reading and Windsor.

The surviving Ledgers of Thomas Sharpe cover the years 1774-1803 and 1819-26. In that period he provided over 1,600 hatchments to almost 200 different people or companies. At one stage he was painting at least one hatchment a week. About 115 of these clients made only up to three orders for hatchments over this period. These were probably the executors of the deceased. One of these customers was called specifically 'the executors of Mrs. Gale'. Members of the Henniker family, who requested six hatchments over the years 1781-1803, five of which were for immediate family, were probably acting in the capacity of executor rather than undertaker. A Mr. George Stewart of Upper Harley Street requested 12 during the period 1790-1798, many for Scottish families and nobility. There is no clue as to his role in making these arrangements.

However, there are some 'companies' to whom hatchments were provided over a long period. One can see company names changing. Mr. Ayscough was a customer in 1776; this later became Ayscough, Wood and Holmes, and Ayscough and Sadler were still buying hatchments in 1825. Ayscough and two other companies (Butler and Thornhill) each commissioned hatchments for over 100 funerals. These 'companies' were not just London based. Heelas and Sons of Wokingham, who had five painted between 1823-1826, is now a High Street shop in Reading and part of the John Lewis Partnership. A summary of the names and occupations of these 'undertakers' is given in Appendix 2.

Thomas Sharpe through his association with the College of Arms did a lot of heraldic work. In addition to making hatchments there was work for armorial china, for seals, painting arms on the backs of chairs and painting banners etc. for the London Livery Companies and the Lord Mayor's Show. The company also carried out the mundane painting and decorating for domestic and commercial premises.

For herald painters outside London it is likely that herald painting was a secondary occupation. No doubt some traded as ordinary painters and coach painters. Richard Chandles of Shrewsbury, *c*.1750, advertised as Armes-Painter and Undertaker.[6] Shrewsbury has more surviving hatchments than any other town, and possibly one or two of these were the product of his work. A century later the company of Holmes and Sons was operating in Derby as coach makers. They also produced hatchments. Several are detailed in the company's work book now in Derby City Library.[7] Some of these hatchments still survive. They include those at

Shepshed, No. 3 (Leicestershire) and Calke Abbey, No. 3 (Derbyshire), (see illustrations 2, 5 and 6). A report of the erection of the hatchment at Shepshed appeared in a local paper as follows:[8]

Hatchment to the Late Charles March Phillipps, Esq. The other day Messrs Holmes and Sons, the celebrated carriage manufacturers, of Derby, erected a hatchment to the late Mr. Phillipps, on the south front of Garendon Hall, near Loughborough, the armorial bearings of which embrace those of the families of March, Lisle, and Phillipps. It is four feet square inside the mourning cloth border, and on a black ground are beautifully emblazoned the family arms of the possessors of Garendon, ... The hatchment, we understand, will eventually be placed in the parish church. The whole has been beautifully executed by Messrs. Holmes's artist, who has the reputation of being the first heraldic painter of the day, and we understand he has been in the employment of that celebrated firm from his youth, covering a space of nearly forty-five years. From this well-known fact, and their extensive connections in the midland counties, they are frequently called upon to paint these sad rememberances of departed friends.

Thomas Sharpe painted hatchments for over 1,600 funerals. For 260 of these events, two hatchments were painted and for 25 three or more hatchments were painted. There are several reasons why two or more hatchments were needed. The principal one was that the person concerned had two or more houses, where it was necessary to display a hatchment (rather than the 17th-century example of a house with two main doors). The funeral items for Mrs. Benyon (1777)[9] clearly state '2 Atchievements for ye two houses'. For Thomas Sharpe many of the families had a London home as well as an estate in the shires. The nobility had more country houses and, therefore, needed more hatchments. Edward, Duke of Norfolk (d.1777) had four painted but even the premier Duke was outdone by the Duchess of Montague, who died in May 1775. There were five painted on her death. (This figure assumes that Thomas Sharpe painted all the hatchments required. It is possible that, with widespread estates, further hatchments could have been painted locally as well as those by Thomas Sharpe in London.)

One aspect of orders for two or more hatchments, for which there appears no obvious explanation, is that the second one may be made a few days after the first one. It is unlikely that this is the result of a repeated oversight. Perhaps the first one went on display at the house from which the funeral started. The second hatchment at the other house was not so important.

When was the hatchment erected at the house? In the majority of cases it seems to have been put up within a few days of death. But there is no firm evidence as to whether this is normally before or after the funeral. In the case of Capt. John Stevens, the coffin maker erected the hatchment the day after the funeral. The records of Thomas Sharpe show that they occasionally provided a man to put up the hatchment. Sir Henry St John Mildmay died 11 November 1808 and two hatchments were erected seven days later at his country estate and his house in London.[10] In this instance they were put up by the undertaker, Charles Smith, Upholsterer.

The putting up of the hatchment would seem to be an agreed process. Thomas Sharpe was required to put up the hatchment for Admiral Leveson-Gower who died in 1792. Additional charges were incurred because the men had to go to Charles Street, Berkeley Square, twice; 'The lady deferring putting up till day after time directed'.

The making of the hatchment had to be done quickly, with the funeral perhaps within a fortnight of the death. There are several examples where Thomas Sharpe apparently was requested to make the hatchment a few days before the death occurred. One must assume that the person had a slow death and the family wanted to be well prepared!

With the production of one hatchment a week some basic frames may have been kept in stock. The trade card of Christopher Gibson, cabinet-maker of St Paul's churchyard, *c.*1710 shows some hatchments hanging on the wall of his premises.[11] These might be blanks but are more likely to be demonstration models for clients to choose from.[12] Some reasonable timescale for the execution of the works must have been required. It is not known why the hatchment of Mr. Dayrell who died in 1790 was made in haste. It incurred a charge of 12s. in addition to the basic price of £1 6s. as 'extra expedition money working late and early and one all night'.

Where two or more are ordered one should not assume that they were identical. It has already been shown from references from the 17th century that even the marshalling could be different. There are two hatchments for Thomas Wentworth Beaumont (d.1848); one at Byworth St Andrew church, the other at Byworth Hall, Northumberland.[13] The Beaumont arms are quarterly in one but alone in the other.

In the later centuries the recorded differences related more to size and decoration than to marshalling. Thomas Sharpe produced three two-yard hatchments for Mr. J. Edmondson for the death of the Duchess of Northumberland in 1776.[14] The one for 'town was gilt with gold and y rest (gilt) with metal'. He also made three for Mr. Ayscough on the death of Sir Joshua Van Neck (No. 1, Huntingfield, Suffolk). Again one frame was gilt with gold.[15]

In some cases it is clear that, where more than one hatchment is produced, one is for the church rather than a second home. Three were ordered for the Earl of Orkney (d.1736), as follows:

> 2 yards square inside the frame for the country
> a yard and a half for the town
> an ell for the church

The Earl of Orkney was a peer and his funeral included a standard and bannerols.[16] There was no request for a shield, crest, helm etc., so possibly the smallest one was put up in the church in their stead. The Marquis of Bath (d.1796)[17] had two achievements a yard and a half square plus a smaller one for the church. The inference is that by 1800 the nobility had their hatchments erected at the church after the funeral instead of putting up their achievements. If this was the case, then a hatchment went up in the church at the same time as that over the door of the house. This practice was followed by the gentry. Two hatchments were produced for Mrs. Hatch, one for the church and one for the house at Chigwell.[18] She was buried at Old Ilford and the hatchments are in churches at Chigwell (No. 9), and Little Ilford (No. 3).

In Scotland two hatchments were used, one at the house and one at the church. For the funeral of Dame Catherine Campbell of Shawfield (1752), the hatchment was put up at the house two days before the funeral. On the morning of the funeral another hatchment was erected on the outside of the church over the door, and was moved inside after the funeral.[19]

The size of the hatchment in the 18th and 19th centuries was probably dictated by two factors. The social or financial status of the deceased and to a lesser extent the space available at the point of display. The above two examples of the Earl of Orkney and the Marquis of Bath show how different sizes of hatchment for the same person were distributed. There were two basic sizes: an ell square (45" by 45"), and a yard and a half square (54" by 54"), with the occasional requirement of one of two yards square.

The nobility tended to use the larger sizes. The following table divides the orders for hatchments painted by Thomas Sharpe between gentry and the peerage and by numbers and size. (Baronets, knights, bishops, generals, admirals etc. are all included with the peers.)

Size	No. painted for each funeral	No. of funerals Gentry	No. of funerals Nobility	Per cent for Nobility
ell	1	908	32	3
ell	2	115	15	11
ell	3	2	1	33
ell	4	0	3	100
y½	1	210	108	32
y½	2	56	74	57
y½	3	0	16	100
y½	4	0	3	100
2 y	1	0	5	100

Table 3. Comparison of the number and size of Hatchments for
Gentry and Peers prepared by Thomas Sharpe.

The work books in the College of Arms for an earlier period
with fewer examples show the same trends.

Normally Thomas Sharpe provided a completed hatchment,
but one entry details what was needed to make one as he provided
only the materials. In January 1776 he provided Mr. Raymond,
Painter of Canterbury, with:

Sundry articles furnished for painting an Atchievement yard and ½ square
viz: 4 books of gold 6s., Cloth 5s., Frame and boards 5s. Painting and
Gilding Do 1s. 6d., Cord for packg. 3d., Black cloth to cover the boards
3s. 6d. Total £1/1/6.

The price of a completed ell hatchment was about £1 12s. 6d.
and that of the yard and a half one at £3 3s. 0d. From 1784 they
were subject to a Government tax (1s. for an ell). The provision of
gilding, extra quarterings, military trophies, arms of more than one
wife all incurred additional charges.

The records of Thomas Sharpe show that virtually every
hatchment had a frame and around this in the majority of cases
were placed boards, many of which were covered with black cloth.
These boards are referred to as early as 1663. The hatchment of
Charles March Philips, in the newspaper cutting above, had a
mourning cloth border. However, the boards seem to have been
discarded if the hatchment was transferred to the church. This is
borne out by the evidence of surviving hatchments in churches.
Also, where a hatchment was made for the church there are no
boards but the frame is broader than normal.

There appear to be two types of frame. One is described as a
'screwed' frame, the other is a 'fast' frame. An order for two

hatchments may specify that one is to be of each type. In 1736 Viscountess Weymouth had two hatchments made with a screwed frame and one with a fast frame. It may be that the later one was for the church.

Some hatchments were painted for the church at the time of the funeral. However there is ample evidence to show that many hatchments hung outside the deceased's house for approximately 12 months before being transferred to the church.[20] Some hatchments had to be repaired or even replaced as the consequence of weathering. Thomas Sharpe erected the hatchment for the Countess de Crequi Canaples at her house in Upper Belgrave Place. Later he took it down, restrained, cleaned and varnished it and put it up in Marylebone church. He also charged for paying the church the appropriate fee.[21] It is not clear in this instance how long the hatchment hung outside the house.

The hatchment of John Stevens, who died 28 April 1777 and was buried 9 May 1777, was provided by Josiah Sarney and erected at Badgemore House on 10 May 1777. No date is given for its repair but this was also carried out by Josiah Sarney before its removal to Wargrave church. The bill of 12s. 6d. for this work was settled on 29 July 1778.[22] Allowing two weeks for the repair and two weeks for the settlement of the account, it seems the hatchment was outside Badgemore House for just over one year. The hatchment of Walter Sneyd at Keele Hall, Staffordshire, was painted by 'Oldfield' of Charles Street, Berkeley Square. Walter Sneyd died on 23 June 1829 and Oldfield took down the hatchment on 1 July 1830.[23] (No indication is given as to its fate.) There are further examples of hatchment repairs which were carried out by Thomas Sharpe about 12 months after the original painting was completed.

The number of hatchments repaired by Thomas Sharpe is small compared with the total number he painted. No doubt some weathered better than others and did not require repair after a year outdoors. However, many would need repair. One might expect that those erected remote from London could have been touched up and cleaned locally by whomever was employed to transfer them from the house to the church. The evidence of John Stevens of Wargrave, Berkshire, and Walter Sneed of Keele Hall, Staffordshire, tends to suggest that this work was referred back to the original makers, even if they were in London.

Some hatchments were painted specifically for the church one year after the death of the deceased. Two hatchments were requested by a Mr. Flower for the death of a Mr. James Cecil of Norfolk Street, The Strand, London, in November 1786.[24] On 20 November 1787 two more were requested by a Mr. Cecil:[25] one was for the church at Walthamstow, Essex, the other for the church at Margate, Kent (Margate, No. 20[26]). Mr. Cecil had died 12 months previously on 18 November 1786,[27] so two hatchments were made one year after his death for erection in the churches. A comparison from some of Thomas Sharpe's work of the dates of death with the dates of the hatchment being commissioned shows that the majority were painted at about the date of death. There are only a few examples which are similar to that of James Cecil quoted above.

One must remember that the transfer of a hatchment to the church does not imply that that church was where the funeral took place. Even though two or more hatchments had been painted for one death, it was impossible for the body to be at two places. The two hatchments for Mr. Cecil above were for two separate churches. However, it is possible for a memorial service to have been held at a second location. Also the introduction of cemeteries from around 1800 may result in the body being laid to rest in the cemetery but the hatchment still being put up in the parish church. Two Berkshire parishes illustrate this point. At Pangbourne all seven members of the Breedon family, whose hatchments hang in the church, had funeral services at the church. At Aldermaston, only three out of the five members of the Congreve family are buried where their hatchments hang.

Thomas Sharpe's ledgers and the work books at the College of Arms show that requirements for the marshalling of arms, the display of trophies, extra shields to display the honour of an Order of Knighthood, or additional marriages, all incurred extra charges. Some work books show that even the shape of the shield was specified. Obviously this all must have been specified and agreed somewhere. It seems that a variety of methods was used to advise the painters of the arms required. One of the few communications from the commissioners to the painters that has been traced is a design for the hatchment of John Tremayne at St Ewe, Cornwall. This consists of a drawing of a shield divided into quarterings. Each quarter is defined by the name of the family together with its blazon.

Many painters must have kept their own 'roll' of arms. The work book of the Holmes family of coach-makers in Derby is very much a local armorial.[28] There is an artist's work book in the

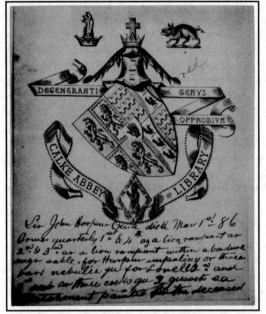

5. Bookplate in work
book of Holmes and
Sons, Coachbuilders,
of Derby used for
preparing the
hatchment of Sir
John Harput Crewe,
9th Bt. D. 1886.
*(Courtesy of Derby
Local Studies
Library; photograph
by J. E. Titterton.)*

British Library which gives the arms of families, arranged county
by county.[29] Thomas Sharpe charged for checking the arms at the
College of Arms, but only in a few instances. Few painters would
have such local access.

There is a reference to the arms being copied from the side
of a carriage in 1849.[30] In another example a sketch is provided
by the deceased's husband.[31] Bookplates were also used. Some
examples of these are found interleaved in the work books at the
College of Arms and in those of Thomas Sharpe. The work book
of Holmes of Derby has a bookplate stuck in it which was used
for the preparation of the hatchment of Sir John Harpur Crewe,
Bt., who died in 1886. The hatchment hangs in Calke Abbey
church. (See illustrations 2, 5 and 6.)

Certainly artists made errors. There are occasional references
in Sharpe to show that single coats were changed to quarterly and
vice versa. However some of these changes seem to be at the
direction of the family. The hatchment of Sir William Wake
(Waltham Abbey, No. 6) was originally painted with the Wake
arms only with Fenton in pretence.[32] Thomas Sharpe had to change
it to quarterly Wake and Drury. The hatchment of Samuel Knight

was painted shortly after his death in November 1823.[33] It was repaired in December 1824, presumably on transfer to the church. In January 1825 it was repainted again, but now with his wife's arms placed in pretence.[34]

Occasionally the arms of a family with a similar sounding surname are used. The hatchment of Sir Sitwell Raresby Sitwell of Renishaw Hall (No. 6), Derbyshire, has the arms of the Earl of Dunmore in pretence. His wife was the daughter of the Earl of Donoughmore. This must be the result of a misunderstanding when the instructions were given. Likewise the hatchment, Upleatham, No. 1 can be identified if the impaled arms of Pennyman are assumed to represent Penn. Some of these 'errors' were deliberate. In 1851 George Bishop produced a hatchment for Thomas Seaton Forman Esq. with the impaled arms of Pembridge (barry of six or and azure on a bend gules three mullets argent). It is stated that the wife's maiden name was known to be Pember but the Pembridge arms were to be used.[35]

Some hatchments have been altered to represent another member of the family. The details of the alterations to the hatchment of Sir James Drax (d.1661), to be used for his son in 1662, are not known. Presumably the impaled arms were changed. One alteration for which there are a number of surviving examples is the changing of a half black background to an all black background on the death of the widow or widower. In some cases this can be deduced from the dates of death of the two people not agreeing with a shield combined with an all black background. In some cases it is quite obvious that although the whole background is black, one can see that half of it is black painted over an originally white background, e.g. Coker Court, East Coker, Somerset.

In 36 years Thomas Sharpe and his successor George Bishop produced nearly 2,000 hatchments, of which only 85 have survived to be recorded in these volumes.[36] For the same period approximately 850 survive in total, so Thomas Sharpe's company was just one of many. From these figures one can estimate that between the years 1700 and 1900 over 100,000 hatchments must have been painted.

Illustrations of hatchments were also used to decorate funeral literature. Trade cards of undertakers and funeral invitations often included hatchments in the design, together with other symbols of mortality and mourning. (See illustration 3.)

6. Hatchment of Sir John Harpur Crewe, 9th Bt. d. 1886. Produced by
Holmes and Sons, Coachbuilders of Derby, hanging at Calke Abbey
Church. *(Photograph by John E. Titterton.)*

It was the sight of Thomas Sharpe's work and that of other
London herald painters which prompted the description in
Thackeray's *Vanity Fair* of Great Gaunt Street, when Becky Sharpe
arrived there. Her carriage 'stopped at a tall gloomy house between
two other tall gloomy houses, each with a hatchment over the
middle drawing-room window; as is the custom in Great Gaunt
Street in which gloomy locality death seems to reign perpetual.'
Hatchments are also depicted in illustrations of church interiors in
Dickens' novels, *Bleak House* and *David Copperfield*. A water-
colour painting by James Miller, 1776, of Cheyne Walk, Chelsea,[37]
shows a hatchment being erected outside the first-floor window
of a house.

The majority of Thomas Sharpe's work was erected outside houses in London. It was impossible for all these hatchments to be transferred to the London churches. Even before the late Victorian church restorations, some churches must have been full to capacity. Most of the surviving work of Thomas Sharpe's artists is to be found in the provinces. (See illustration 4 and Appendix 3)

From their first appearance until about 1850 the use of hatchments had increased continuously, so that it was a common sight, especially in London. Hatchments, after being displayed outside a house for perhaps a year, were cleaned, repaired and even replaced before being transferred to a church. Village churches would show generation after generation of the local squires whilst those in the towns would display those of their gentry and wealthy citizens. (There are over 50 hatchments in Shrewsbury.) The fact that they were taken for granted as ordinary items of everyday life and death has meant that little documentary account of them has survived. The accession of Queen Victoria saw their use at its height.

1. See illustration 3 for trade card of W. Barton, who describes himself as Upholsterer, Cabinet-Maker, Appraiser, Auctioneer, Paper-Hanger and Undertaker.
2. Guildhall Library, Ms 5871.
3. Berkshire Record Office, D/Esv(M) F25.
4. Berkshire Record Office, D/Esv(M) F31/48.
5. Guildhall Library Ms 546/1 and 546/2. The two documents are ledgers of Thomas Sharpe and his successor George Bishop and they detail the output both heraldic and routine for the years 1774-1803 and 1819-26.
6. Litten, J., *op cit.*, p.133 and fig.3.
7. Derby City Local Studies Library, Ms 9555.
8. This is transcribed from a photocopy of the article. Unfortunately the newspaper was not identified.
9. Berkshire Record Office, D/EBy F20.
10. Bodleian Library, John Jackson Collection, Bill Headings, Vol. 24.
11. Litten, J., *op cit.*, p.25.
12. There is an undertaker's demonstration hatchment recorded in Chapter 8, No. 18 of the miscellaneous section.
13. See Vol. 3 of this series.
14. Ledgers of Thomas Sharpe, Vol. 2 114.
15. Ledgers of Thomas Sharpe, Vol. 1 32.
16. See Appendix 1, No. 1.9 for details of the items requested.

17. Ledgers of Thomas Sharpe, Vol. 2 71v.
18. Ledgers of Thomas Sharpe, 2 79v.
19. Burnett, C. J., *op cit.*
20. Illustration 2 shows the hatchment of Sir John Harpur Crewe, 9th Bt.,
     hanging at Calke Abbey.
21. Ledgers of Thomas Sharpe, 2 f 68.
22. Berkshire Record Office, D/Esv(M) F28.
23. Keele University Library, Sneyd papers, 3447.
24. Ledgers of Thomas Sharpe, 1 138v.
25. Ledgers of Thomas Sharpe, 1 151v.
26. The design of this hatchment is recorded in College of Arms Work
     Book 1786-8. The blazons of the arms of the two wives match
     those of the hatchment at Margate.
27. *Gentleman's Magazine.*
28. Derby City Local Studies Library, Ms 9555.
29. British Library, Add Ms 19817.
30. College of Arms, Painter's Work Book, 1848-52 f.40v.
31. College of Arms, Painter's Work Book, 1848-52 f.79.
32. Ledgers of Thomas Sharpe, 1 139 v.
33. Ledgers of Thomas Sharpe, 2 25 v.
34. The hatchment for a Mrs. Fitch, painted in 1794, had the impaled
     arms changed to pretence in 1796; College of Arms Work Book
     1788-96. It has not been proved that these ladies became heiresses
     posthumously.
35. College of Arms, Painter's Work Book, 1848-52, f.80.
36. These are recorded in Appendix 3. There will be other hatchments by
     this company for the years where the ledgers have not survived.
37. Victoria and Albert Museum.

Chapter 5

A Gradual Decline

The practice of painting and hanging hatchments in churches has continued into the 1990s but is now at a very low level. The gradual decline began in the mid-19th century and one might suggest that the practice, as a routine display of mourning, ended with the First World War, if not earlier. To establish the reasons for this decline may well require consideration of the changing nature of the Landed Gentry in this period, and also changes in the Church of England.

The decline is evident from the number of surviving examples from this period. Possibly the number of hatchments being painted was initially the same, but was there now some problem with the transfer to the church after the due period of display outside the deceased's home? The separate introductions to several county lists in previous volumes of this series refer to the loss of a large number of hatchments from churches at the time of Victorian restorations. Once these restorations were complete, was there likely to be encouragement to recommence the practice in the church? Likewise, if the local lord of the manor had agreed or accepted the removal of a number of his ancestors' hatchments, and possibly contributed to the restoration costs of the church, he was perhaps less inclined to continue the tradition even if the hatchment was still erected at the house.

The reluctance of the incumbent to agree to the erection of new hatchments may go deeper. John Charles Cox in *English Church Fittings, Furniture and Accessories* (1907), writes:

> Happily the recent revival of the proper use to which a church should be put has put to flight hatchments within a church, and probably no incumbent could nowadays be found to admit such a thing.

This may be an exaggeration of the attitude of the clergy but the long term effects of the Oxford Movement must be considered as a possible factor in the process of decline.

Hatchments were not alone in this decline. Church monuments suffered similarly but perhaps a little later. Professor Brian Kemp in *English Church Monuments* (1980), discussing the erection of church monuments at the end of the 19th century, wrote:

> The practice of erecting grand monuments in churches was itself in decline by then and was destined to virtually disappear in the course of the twentieth century. For some decades before 1900 people had increasingly been chosen to be commemorated by stained glass windows or by church fittings, rather than by (grand) monuments.

This changing attitude to the erection of hatchments in the churches seems to have resulted in two new practices for using hatchments.

One is the practice of painting a 'family' hatchment, which could be re-used for successive members of the family. These, it seems, would display only the main family arms and would have either dexter background black or sinister background black, presumably to cover all options.

This is referred to in correspondence prompted by a letter published in the *Sunday Times* from Sir Frank Watney K.C.V.O., in 1950. Sir Picton Bagge Bt. replied as follows:

> I am writing to let you know that my family has two hatchments, one for the head of the family and one for his wife (or widow). On their deaths the appropriate hatchment is placed over the outside door of the South porch, where the coffin lies on the night before the funeral. They have been in the family beyond the memory of anyone living. In my lifetime they have been used on the death of my father (1916), of my mother (1918), and my elder brother (1939). The coats of arms are painted on canvas and mounted on wood.[1]

(The hatchments still survive.)

The letter implies that this practice went back into the 19th century. If this is the case, it could explain the problems of identifying a few hatchments which display the family arms only but have a half black background. Some of them may be explained by non-armigerous wives but, where the rank and identity of the family can be established, some of the later ones must be for people with armigerous wives, e.g. 1st Baron Amherst at Riverhead, Kent, and No. 3 at Elvenham Hall, Hampshire, for a Baron Calthorpe.

The second practice is that of re-using an old hatchment with incorrect arms. Another reply to Sir Frank's letter, from a Mr. Hassall, is quite specific that this took place at Hallaton, Leicestershire, in 1931 on the death of R. H. Price-Dent Esq.[2] The old hatchment was restored and displayed for a period of two weeks and then returned to the church. In 1953 on the death of Lady Ashburnham the hatchment of her grandmother was hung over the door of Ashburnham House.

There are 112 recorded hatchments for the 20th century. Many of them are at churches where hatchments for earlier family members are on display. However, the latter part of the 20th century has seen the rise of what one might call posthumous hatchments. These are hatchments painted some time after the death of the person commemorated and then put up at the church without being displayed at the house. The hatchment is being used as a memorial.

7. Procession at the memorial service of Humphrey D. Lindsay MA at St Mary, Hemel Hempstead, Saturday 3 November 1990.
(Photograph by Frame One, Hemel Hempstead.)

This practice is not new. Two hatchments in Vol.2, p.135 are for people who died in 1619 and 1622 respectively, but the hatchments are considered to be of a much later date. The same applies to four of the hatchments of the Chadwick family at Mavesyn Ridware, Staffordshire. Recent examples of these posthumous hatchments include those at Chelsea Old Church, Broxted, and Chirk.

The Canadian Heraldry Society recently supervised the erection of an hatchment in Ottawa Cathedral. It was for a previous President of the Society. The hatchment at Broxted was put up for Mrs. Shirley McCarthy in 1990. She died in 1987 while her son was a hostage in Lebanon. The hatchment was dedicated to her at a service in 1991.

The hatchment of Humphrey D. R. Lindsay at Hemel Hempstead follows more closely the old tradition. He was headmaster at Gadebridge Park, 1932-62 and Westbrook Hay School, 1963-7, Hemel Hempstead. The hatchment was painted by Mr. M. W. C. Holmes of Shrewsbury, who bore it aloft on a pole in a procession to the church at the memorial service held on 3 November 1990. In that procession pupils at the school bore his bible, *Book of Common Prayer*, and academical robes. After the service the hatchment was hung at the school. It is hoped to transfer it to the church. With these items and the hatchment carried in the procession, the occasion must have echoed in a small way the Tudor events outlined in the first chapter of this book. (See illustration 6.)

1. See Appendix 4 for transcripts of this and other relevant letters.
2. See Appendix 4. The hatchment at Hallaton is for a Thwaites-Den marriage and is unidentified.

Chapter 6

Features of the Hatchment

1. Its size and construction

Hatchments in the 17th century tended to be smaller than those of later centuries. Early examples varied from between 12 inches square to one yard and a quarter square, and they were invariably painted on wood. In the 18th and 19th centuries they became standardised in two sizes, a yard and a quarter square, called an ell square, and a yard and a half square. Examples of smaller hatchments do exist but they are very much the exception. Records still exist of hatchments of two metres square, made for one or two members of the nobility. Only one or two examples exist where the hatchment is not square, i.e. the angles are not right angles, e.g. Thorncombe, Dorset.

Eighteenth- and nineteenth-century hatchments tend to be painted on canvas. There are exceptions. The hatchments of Sir John Eardley Eardley-Wilmot who died in 1849 at Berkswell, and those for Francis Gregory and Arthur Francis Gregory at Stivichall, Warwickshire, are painted on the backs of house floor-cloths.[1] Those surviving examples painted on silk are unlikely to be hatchments intended to be hung outside the house for a period of time, though possibly they are 'Majestie' escutcheons carried at the funerals or they may be pulpit hatchments. The canvas hatchment is normally surrounded by a wooden frame which is painted black or covered with black cloth. The frame of the hatchment of Ralph Sneyd of Keele, Staffordshire, in 1737 was covered with black 'flannel'.[2] It is later simply termed 'black cloth'.

The frame in many cases was surrounded by boards, but in England, few, if any, examples have survived. The Thomas Sharpe ledgers suggest that boards were not required if a hatchment was being put up inside a church. The frames for church hatchments were slightly broader. Many are decorated in gold with symbols of mortality such as skulls, crossbones, hour glasses and cherubs' heads.[3]

2. The Marshalling of Arms

The marshalling of the achievement on a hatchment in most respects followed the normal rules of heraldry. The hatchments of bachelors, husbands (i.e. wife surviving) and widowers were displayed on a shield with crest and mantling. For a wife (i.e. husband surviving) the arms were still displayed upon a shield but surmounted by the lover's knot or cherub's head. Widows' and spinsters' arms were displayed on lozenges and again surmounted by the lover's knot or cherub's head. There is, however, an early example in Marnhull, Dorset, for a lady where a crest surmounts a lozenge. This is thought to be for the spinster daughter of Sir Lewis Dive.

The display of multiple quarterings was very popular in the late 17th century and, although some arms do display more, the majority after 1700 are plain arms or quarterly of four. The most notable exception to this is the hatchment for Lt. Gen. Sir Love Parry Jones-Parry at Llanbedrog in Wales. This has 63 quarterings.

Military trophies are to be found on the hatchments of generals and admirals. The award of an honour K.G., K.T., K.B., K.M.G. to an individual may result in two oval shields accolé. The dexter displayed the knight's or peer's arms within a ribbon of the Order whilst the sinister oval showed his arms impaling those of his wife or wives. Where the individual had more than one decoration then all were usually shown below the dexter shield. In such cases the partial black background may have been adjusted to be in line as far as was practical, with the impalement line of the sinister shield.[4] The hatchment at Sidestrand, Norfolk, for Samuel, 1st Viscount Templewood (d.1959), is unique in that both husband and wife were honoured and each shield has a badge below it.

The arms of a husband and wife are normally impaled. Where there was a marriage to an heiress, the wife's arms are placed on an escutcheon of pretence. The conventions of dexter background black, or sinister background black, were still followed even though the arms of the wife did not occupy the sinister half of the shield.

On some hatchments the arms of an heiress wife were both impaled and placed in pretence. The number of examples is not great, with only 20 or so dated examples. All but one, dated 1671, are for the period 1700-66. Examples are also to be found on tombs in the same period. It would seem that this practice was one of artistic fashion rather than obeying an heraldic or genealogical requirement as there are also over 90 examples of hatchments with the arms of an heiress wife in pretence only.

The wish to show the arms of two or more wives on a hatchment has produced several practices. Some, as far as a matter of heraldic display, have advantages over others. There were two main methods used in the late 17th century. One gave reasonable prominence to the arms of the husband and provided a practical shape for the display of the arms of the wife.

The husband's were displayed in a central shield with two smaller shields at the sides. These smaller shields displayed the arms of the husband marshalled with those of his wives, either in pretence or impaled. The first wife's arms were on the shield to the dexter and the second wife's arms on the shield to the sinister. Usually each of the smaller shields had its own dexter black/sinister black/all black background display. Early examples of this form show the small shields painted as depicting small square canvases (with escutcheons painted on them) pinned or stuck to the main canvas. This may indicate the practical origin of this form of display. Such an arrangement has further advantages if the male arms contain several quarterings. It was the most popular method of showing two marriages during the 17th and 18th centuries and shared the honours with two other methods in the 19th centuries.

This method was perhaps the only practical one for Henry Boulton, of Moulton, Lincolnshire, who died in 1828, and who had been married five times. His arms impaling those of his fifth and last wife are on the shield in the centre. His arms are marshalled with each of those of his first four wives on four smaller shields displayed in each corner of the hatchment.

The other method employed was to divide the shield per pale into three sections to accommodate the arms of the husband and his two wives. The husband's arms would be placed in the centre with the arms of the first and second wives to the dexter and sinister respectively. Examples of this date from the latter half of the 17th century but were most common in the first half of the 19th century.

A variation on this practice was to place the husband's arms to the dexter with the first wife's arms in the centre and the second wife's arms to the sinister. One consequence of this is that, with a hatchment with three arms per pale, one cannot immediately decide which are the arms of the husband. This latter, and less popular, of the two variations described is heraldically more correct in that the arms of both wives are to the sinister of the husband's.

Some husbands took this one step further in that their own arms occupied the dexter half of the shield with the sinister half divided per pale. Each wife only had a quarter of the shield and the arms were very long and thin. A reasonable display of arms, containing three charges 2 and 1, became very difficult (see photograph for Dorset, Vol. 8).

The desire for the male arms to have a sufficiently prominent display, i.e. half of the shield rather than being lost or confused with the arms of his two wives, may have led to the final method. In this situation the husband's arms occupied the dexter half of the shield. The sinister half was divided per fess. The first wife's arms were placed in chief and the second wife's in base. This gave a better arrangement for the display of the arms involved. It was popular in the 19th century and became the most used form in the latter half of that century.

The usual practice for a man who had made two marriages, one of which was to an heiress, was to have only one shield with the arms of the heiress placed in pretence and the arms of the other wife impaled. Other arrangements suggest the order of the marriage; in this arrangement the heiress wife could have been the first or second wife. The 11th Duke of Norfolk married twice, on both occasions to heiresses, and he had two escutcheons of pretence (see Arundel, Sussex and Holme Lacy, Herefordshire).

The above discussion has considered arrangements for a man who had married twice. There are a few examples of the arms of three wives being included in the arrangement. There are several examples of ladies who had married twice. Each of the three methods outlined above has been used.

There is one further method used where a lady had married twice. This is where two separate lozenges were displayed, one for each marriage. This was employed where the husbands were of different rank and there was a desire to display supporters and coronets appropriate to the rank. Examples of this can be found at Harefield, Middlesex,[5] and Stoke Poges, Buckinghamshire. The latter is interesting in that the arms of Howard appear twice with different difference marks. The lady's husbands were Howard first cousins, one an Earl the other a Knight. At Haselbeach, Northamptonshire, the marshalling of the arms on the hatchment of George Savil Foljambe includes the arms of both his wives and the arms of his second wife's first husband!

Examples of situations where a husband and wife were divorced are few. It would seem the arms of the wife were simply ignored. One example is for the 12th Duke of Norfolk at Arundel.

Hatchments exist for the situation where a member of an armigerous family had married someone who was not armigerous. Generally the arms impale a plain or diapered argent blank. A rare example is at Westleigh, Devon (No. 4), where the wife was armigerous and the husband was not. Technically, illegitimate children were not armigerous and, therefore, should be dealt with in a like manner. There are examples where illegitimate daughters of peers used their father's arms. At Stoke Poges the arms of the 8th Duke of Leeds impale a blank. His wife, Harriet, was the illegitimate daughter of the 1st Earl of Granville and Lady Bessborough.

A further marshalling arrangement to be considered is that where the arms of office were impaled with those of the individual. The arms of office displayed on hatchments include those of an archbishop, bishop, dean, or warden of a school or college. They normally occupy the dexter half of the shield. The majority are for wardens of Oxford colleges, with some examples at Cambridge, Eton and Winchester. The earliest examples are for Archbishop Abbot in Guildford, 1633, and John Barwick,[6] Dean of St Paul's (d.1664); the next one is dated 1783. They were more common in the 19th century with only six in the 20th century.

There has been some discussion as to the correct colour of the background to the arms of office. Archbishop Abbot had sinister background black and Dean Barwick had all background black. With few exceptions the rest had a white background behind the arms of office. At St John's, Cambridge, the hatchment of The Very Rev. James Wood, Master of the College and Dean of Ely Cathedral, has his personal arms impaling to the dexter the arms of the college with the arms of the Deanery of Ely to the sinister. Only his personal arms have a black background. The theory is that the office does not die and thus should have a white background. However, the opinion of Mr. H. Stanford London, *Norfolk Herald Extraordinary*, was that the arms of office are borne by the individual as an augmentation of Honour and are thus part of his personal arms.[7] Therefore, such hatchments could have an all black background quite correctly.

There are some examples where an individual who held office was also married. Then, either two shields are displayed with the dexter showing the arms of office impaling the individual's arms and the sinister showing the individual's arms impaling those of his wife or, one shield shows all three arms impaled, the office to the dexter, the husband in the centre and the wife to the sinister. This practice is used even when the hatchment is that of the wife with the husband surviving.

The study of the early hatchments has shown two cases where the arms of an heiress wife were included as a quartering of the husband's arms. At old St Chad's, Shrewsbury a hatchment for Sir Vincent Corbet Kt., who died in 1622, has been identified from the initials S. V. C. K. He was the only Vincent of the family who was a knight and not a baronet. One of the arms quartered Humfreston However, it was he who married the Humfreston heiress. Likewise the hatchment of Sir George Wintour, Bt. at Cumberland Lodge Windsor, has the arms of Kempe as the 2nd quarter. Again it was Sir George who married the Kempe heiress. One could argue that the Corbet hatchment may have been altered to be used for a male descendant. This cannot explain Sir George Wintour's hatchment He was the first and last baronet and had no children. Were both these hatchments painted incorrectly or altered subsequently, or are they examples of a Stuart marshalling practice which was short lived?

3. The diamond shape

The most recognisable feature about a hatchment is its diamond shape. Diamond-shaped armorial boards are found in the Low Countries, where they were used before they were used in England The shape would, therefore, seem to have been introduced from the Low Countries. One still needs to consider the reason for its introduction on the continent. The answer may be that the diamond shape was a 'fashionable' shape for framing designs when these panels were first developed.

The use of the diamond shape can be traced throughout the 16th century both in England and the Low Countries in a variety of media. The most common one is brass. (This might be because brass is one of the more durable forms and because it is one of the best recorded.) Table three details some examples.

One can see that the trend was for the shape to enclose figures and other items for the first half of the century and only armorial designs for the second half. (Illustration 7.)

In the 17th century the use of the diamond shape went out of fashion. It continued in the Low Countries in hatchments and armorial panels possibly because it was a practical shape for its function. If someone was required to carry a board in a procession a diamond shape was easier for one person to handle and

Date	Medium	Person	Location	Armorial only
1396	Brass	Machtet Roelants	formerly Great Beguinage, Louvain	No
1512	Brass	Jehan de Tonguen	St Jacques, Bruges	No
1529	Brass	Margaret Hronebolt (born in Ghent)	Fulham, Middlesex	No
1544	Brass	John Leigh	Addington, Surrey	Yes
1550	Brass	Adrian, Grandson of Bartholomew Roeland	Breda, Holland	No
1553	Brass	Nicholas Saunders	Charlwood, Surrey	Yes
1557	Brass	Jane Seynt John	Thornton, Bucks.	Yes
1559	Brass	John Corbet	Sprowston, Norfolk	Yes
1570	Table Carpet	Royal Arms	Gorhambury House St Albans	Yes
1580	Monument	Sir John Horsey	Sherborne Abbey	Yes

Table 3. Examples of the use of the diamond shape before 1600.

control. Likewise, if the device was to be hung from a building, the diamond shape was easier and more practical to suspend. A square board subject to the wind and rain could become skewed quickly. The diamond shape tends to be self correcting.

8. Part of the brass of Nicholas Saunders, d. 1553 at Charlwood church, Surrey. *(Brass rubbing by J. E. Titterton.)*

4. The black and white background to the arms

The use of an all black or half black and half white background behind the arms is the second feature which is distinctive of an hatchment. The theory is quite simple. Hugh Clark and Thomas Wormull, Engravers, explained it quite clearly in 'A short Essay and Introduction to Heraldry, 1776'.

> 'By the following rules, may be made known upon sight of any hatchment, what the person was when living, whether a private gentleman or knight, by the helmet; if a nobleman, by the coronet; whether a married man, batchelor, or widower or whether a married woman, maid, or widow, &c.
>
> 1. When a batchelor dies, his arms and crest are painted single or quartered, but never impaled; the ground of the hatchment under the shield is all black.
>
> 2. When a maiden dies, her arms (but no crest) must be placed in a lozenge, and may be single or quartered, with the ground under the escutcheon all black, as the former.
>
> 3. When a married man dies, his arms are impaled with his wife's the ground of the hatchment under his side of the shield, is black, the ground under his wife's side is white; the black side signifies the husband to be dead, and the wife living.
>
> 4. When a married woman dies, her arms being impaled with her husband's (but no crest) the ground of the hatchment under her side of the shield is black, that of her husband white, which signifies the wife to be dead and the husband living.
>
> 5. When a widower dies, his arms are impaled with those of his wife with crest; the ground of the hatchment to be all black.
>
> 6. When a widow dies her arms are impaled with her husband's in a lozenge (but no crest) the ground of the hatchment to be all black.
>
> 7. When a man is the last of a family, the death's head supplying the place of the crest, denoting that death has conquered all.
>
> 8. When a woman is the last of a family her arms are placed in a lozenge with a death's head on the top of the field.

The use of the background on hatchments according to these rules was observed from around 1700. The situation prior to this date is not very clear. Work books at the College of Arms show that the half black/white background was used on funeral escutcheons in the early part of the 17th century. It was used on the rectangular board at Lydiard Tregoze and dated 1628. However, the earliest surviving diamond-shaped hatchment with the impaled arms of husband and wife with a partial white background was in

1648 at Preshute, Wiltshire. Further examples followed in the second half of the century, but it is clear that there are some hatchments with impaled arms and an all black background, where there was a surviving partner. These include the hatchments for Viscount Savage (d.1635), Long Melford, Suffolk, Sir John Hobart (d.1647), privately owned (Vol. 2), and the 11th Earl of Northumberland (d.1670), Tadcaster, Yorkshire.

One can conclude that hatchments originally had an all black background and that the partial black and white background was an English development taken from other aspects of heraldic funeral work. The hatchments in the Low Countries rarely have a split background. In an article on Painted Heraldic Panels by Messrs. Bayley and Steer[8] it was stated that, there, a black background was used for a married person and a white background for a single person. No examples of a white background, at least for a single person (see Temple Newsam, No. 1, Yorkshire) have been recorded.

The source of this practice may lie in the philosophy and art of the period. The painting by John Souch of the death of the wife of Thomas Aston (1635) shows Thomas Aston with his son alongside a bed.[9] In the bed is his deceased wife's mortal body and his wife's soul in human form kneeling alongside the bed. At the top of the painting is a shield showing the arms of Aston impaling those of his wife. These arms are on a square board which is fixed to the tester of the bed. The background around the shield is decorated with two laurel sprigs. The dexter half is painted light green with the laurel having light green foliage. The sinister half is dark green with dark green foliage. The immediate effect is similar to that on hatchments, a light (white) background to the arms of the living and a dark (black) background to the arms of the deceased. (Illustration 1.)

Closer examination reveals the conceit of this part of the painting. The dark green leaves are healthy leaves because Mrs. Aston now enjoys everlasting life. The light green laurel leaves are light in colour because they are withering. Thomas Aston is still trapped in the mortal world! It has already been demonstrated that the room where the deceased lay was heraldically decorated. Whilst an armorial board of some kind will have been used, the purpose of the board shown in this painting and its decoration may be assumed to identify the people in the painting and to be part of the symbolism of everlasting life.

The background to the arms on this picture poses a number of questions. The light and dark green background apparently has some connection with the black and white background of hatchments. But which came first? At the time the painting was made, the half black and half white background was already in use on some funeral heraldry. Did funeral painters see early examples of this kind of symbolism and adapt it for funeral heraldry and then to hatchments, or did the portrait artist see funeral heraldry and adapt it to display the idea of everlasting life after death?

A similar treatment can be found on an early 16th-century armorial table carpet of the Luttrell family.[10] It displays three coats of arms with a patterned framework. This pattern is modified around each shield; one has an all black background, one has an all terracotta background, and the third has a half terracotta/half black background.[11] Genealogically this can be dated to between 1514 and 1522.[12] This carpet shows that the half light/half dark background, to show living and dead partners, was established long before black and white were used on hatchments.

Possibly hatchment painters adopted the idea from seeing its symbolic use by artists of the period such as John Souch. Perhaps they combined the idea with that of using black and white on hatchments of the Low Countries, rather than light and dark shades.

As with the origin of the diamond shape, the use of the background to indicate a surviving partner may well be an idea that developed over a period of time rather than immediately.

5. Mottoes

The majority of the hatchments have a motto written below the arms. Occasionally one may be found above the arms with the crest but this is normally where the motto is associated with the crest. Initially the family motto was used but by 1700 a motto expressing a sentiment relating to death and life after death started to be used. The most common ones in this category are: *Resurgam, Mors Januae Vitae* and *In Coelo Quies. Mors Januae Vitae* (Death is the gateway to life) was popular in the first half of the 18th century; its sentiment was similar to the symbolism of the Souch painting above. It was soon pushed into second place by *In Coelo Quies* whose popularity continued well into the 1800s. *Resurgam* appeared regularly from around 1780 and soon became the most popular of the three.

There has been some argument as to whether the translation of *Resurgam* should be the first person future, 'I shall arise', or the first person subjunctive 'Let me arise'. There are 11 examples of its use in the plural. Only one is subjunctive, *resurgamus*: the other 10 are future, *resurgemus*. The conclusion must be that *Resurgam* should be read in the future tense.

The use of these mottoes prompted the composition of the following lines:

> Whene'er a hatchment we discern (a truth before ne'er started)
> The motto surely makes us learn the sex of the departed
> If the husband sleeps, he deems death's day a 'felix dies'
> Of unaccustomed quiet dreams and cries 'In coelo quies'
> But if the wife's, she from the grave wounds Parthian like 'post tergum'
> Hints to her spouse his future doom and threat'ning cries
> 'Resurgam'. [13]

By 1830 one hatchment in three used *Resurgam* with fewer than 50 per cent being painted with the family motto. The decline in the use of the hatchment saw an even quicker decline in the use of this kind of motto. After 1875 the family motto was used on at least 75 per cent of all hatchments.[14]

6. Crest, mantling and supporters

The crests used on hatchments for men follow the normal use as displayed on other heraldic achievements. The crest is placed above the arms and in such a position may be found across the division between a black and white background. Where the tincture of the crest is principally black or white then the division of the background may be diverted around the crest so that it can be displayed clearly (see photograph of St Helens 5, Vol. 7). If the hatchment was painted for a lady then a true lover's knot or a cherub's head will be placed at the top of the hatchment in the place of a crest.

The use of mantling or a mantle for peers and supporters follows the normal heraldic practices. The only exception is that the mantling is normally gules and argent. The use of the two principal colours from the coat is not common practice.

7. Shield shape

Hatchments provide a record of heraldic art for nearly three centuries. Unfortunately it has not proved practical to carry out an analysis on the use of shield shapes. However, it is known from some herald

painters' note books that the shape of the shield was specified
Therefore one may expect to find examples of one shape being use
some time after it had been superceded by another shape.

1. Country House Floors, 1987.
2. Keele University Library, Sneyd Archives.
3. See photograph for Berkshire in Vol. 4.
4. Compare the photographs for Kent and Sussex in Vol. 5.
5. See the Photograph for Middlesex in Vol 6.
6. See photograph for Northumberland in Vol 3.
7. Mr. Stanford London explained this in a paper in 1951, which i
    produced in Appendix 4.
8. Bayley and Bliss, *op cit.*
9. Manchester City Art Galleries.
10. Burrell Museum, Glasgow.
11. I am grateful to Mr. Keith Lovell for drawing my attention to thi
    carpet and the treatment of the background behind the arms.
12. Research by Mr. Keith Lovell.
13. Quoted from Smith, C. J., 'Funeral Hatchments', *Country Life* —
    July 1952.
14. This analysis is base on an index to the mottoes used on hatchment
    prepared by Mr. Bass, Tylers Mead, Dereham Rd, Reepham
    Norfolk. Mr. Bass intends to deposit a copy in the Heraldry Societ
    Library.

Chapter 7

Hatchments of Ireland and former British Colonies

The title of the Survey is 'Hatchments in Britain'. Hatchments are also found outside the British Isles. This section details those hatchments reported in other English-speaking countries where it is clear that they are following a British practice.

This part of the Survey cannot be as complete as that of the British Isles. It has not been practical to investigate the churches of all the former British Colonies. The main collections are in Canada, Ireland and the United States of America.

Few of those recorded in the United States survive today. Some have been destroyed and others have simply disappeared. However, they do show that the practice was continued by colonial families after leaving England. A painting of 1768 of a colonial house in Boston, Massachusetts shows a hatchment hanging below the central dormer window.[1]

Some references to hatchments in the United States are to items which are not hatchments. In the 18th century young ladies, as part of their education, embroidered family arms on diamond-shaped panels of black silk. However these had no funeral nor mourning purpose.

Several hatchments in Ireland are not true hatchments. At Kinsale four out of five contain inscriptions and at Cashell Cathedral all six are late 20th-century paintings for earlier individuals.

The editors would be pleased to learn of any future discoveries.

9. Hatchment of Edward Hill, d. 1706 at the Shirley Plantation, Virginia, U.S.A.
(Courtesy of the Shirley Plantation.)

AUSTRALIA
SYDNEY, St James' Church

1. Dexter 2/3 background black

Two oval shields, Dexter within ribbon of the Order of St Michael and St George   Vert a fess dancetty ermine between in chief a stag's head cabossed and in base two escallop shells or (Duff)   Sinister within a garland of laurel leaves   Duff, impaling, Or (brown) three lions' heads erased gules (for Scott)

Crest: A demi lion gules holding in its paw a sword proper pommel and hilt or   Mantling: Gules and argent   Motto: Virtute et opera

Supporters: Two sailors proper habited in white waistcoats and breeches, blue jacket, black tie and hat, black shoes with gold buckles, black belt with gold buckle and gold knee bands and holding in their exterior hand a sword proper pommel and hilt or   Inscription on frame 'The right Honourable Sir Robert William Duff C.C.M.G. Governor 1893-1895'.

For the Right Honourable Sir Robert William Duff of Fetteresso, who m. Louisa, youngest dau. of Sir William Scott of Ancrum, Bt.

He was Governor of New South Wales 1893-95 and d. in Sydney 15 March 1895.   (B.L.G. 1937 ed.).

CANADA
HALIFAX St Paul's Cathedral (Nova Scotia)

1. Buff background

Azure a lion rampant argent (Durell)

Crest: From a ducal coronet or a saracen's head affonté proper

Mantling: Gules and argent (leaf design)   Motto: Fidelis et generosus

Inscribed on the lower boards of the frame 'Admiral Philip Durell' in base '1766'.

For Admiral Philip Durell d. 1766 who was with General Wolfe at Quebec.

2. Buff background

Argent a cross raguly gules (Lawrence)

Crest: A pike's tail proper   Mantling: Gules and argent (leaf design)

Inscribed on the lower boards of the frame 'Govenor [sic] Charles Lawrence' in base '1770'.

For Governor Charles Lawrence, d. 1770.

3. All black background
Argent two bars azure (Parr)
Crest: An arm in armour holding a pair of compasses proper
Mantling: Gules and argent (leaf design)
Inscribed on the lower boards of the frame 'Govenor [sic] John Parr', in
base '1781'.
For Governor John Parr, d. 1781.

4. Buff background
Azure a saltire argent over all an escutcheon or (Morris)
Crest: Above a ring a mullet or all above a small scroll argent, the
background of the ring being per pale sable and azure
Mantling: Gules and argent (Leaf design)
Inscribed on the lower boards of the frame 'Hon Charles Morris Surveyor
General', and in base '1781'.
For Hon Charles Morris, Surveyor General, d. 1781.

5. Buff background
Qly, 1st, Argent a lion rampant gules, 2nd, Gules a tower proper, 3rd,
Argent a galley sails furled sable in base a salmon naiant proper, 4th, Or
a hand couped in fess gules holding a cross crosslet fitchy (McLean)
Crest: Two branches (laurel ?) in saltire proper and an axe erect
Mantling: Gules and argent (leaf pattern)   Mottoes: Above the
crest, Altera merces   Below shield, Virtus duressima terit
Inscribed on the lower boards of the frame 'Brigadier General Francis
McLean' and in base '1782'
For Brigadier General Francis McLean, d. 1782.

6. Buff background
Gules lions combattant or supporting a sword proper (Finucane)
Crest: A falcon rising argent   Mantling: Gules and argent (leaf
design)   Motto: Fide et fortitudine vivo
Inscribed on the lower boards of the frame 'Chief Justice Bryan
Finucane', in base '1785'.

7. Buff background
Sable on a chevron between three bulls' heads erased or a pair of
dividers proper (Bulkeley)
Crest: Out of a ducal coronet or a bull's head argent cabossed or
Mantling: Gules and argent (leaf pattern)
Inscribed on the lower boards of the frame 'Hon Richard Bulkeley
Provincial Secretary', in base '1800'.
For Hon Richard Bulkeley, Provincial Secretary, d. 1800.

There is a further diamond shaped board. This is all wooden with the
arms carved on it; possibly for a German baron.

LUNENBURG St John's Church (Nova Scotia)

Two hatchments reported here in 1952 but there are no details available.

OTTAWA   Christ Church Cathedral

1. All black background

Azure on a bend argent between in chief a maple leaf and in base a
naval crown or three escallops gules (Pullen)
Crest: A pelican in her piety or charged on the body with a maple leaf
gules   Mantling: Gules and argent   Motto: Nulla pallescere culpa
Pendant below the arms is the Gold Medal of the Royal Canadian
Geographical Society
Inscription on the frame 'Capt. Thomas Charles Pullen O.C., C.D., D.Sc,
R.C.N Artic Pathfinder Born 27 May 1918 Died 3 Aug. 1990'
For Captain Thomas C. Pullen President of the Heraldry Society of
Canada 1971-1973 and d. 3 Aug 1990. (Heraldry in Canada, September
1992)
(Artwork by Gordon Macpherson)

INDIA
TRICHINOPOLY, Christ Church

1. All black background

Ermine three bulls statant or (Horne)
Crest: On a wreath argent and sable a bull's head or   No mantling
Motto: Be firm
For Brigadier General Matthew Horne of Hon E.I.Co. who m. Miss Anne
Selman (d. 1774) and d. 14 Dec 1774.   (Recorded 1957)

IRELAND
ADARE (Limerick)

1. All black background

Vert a pegasus passant ermine a chief or (Quin)
Earl's Coronet   Mantle: Gules and argent   Motto: Quae sursum
volo videre   Supporters: Two ravens proper wings elevated collared
and chained or
For Richard, 1st Viscount Adare and Earl of Dunraven, who d. 24 Aug
1824.   (G.E.C.)

BANGOR (Down)

In private possession

1. All black background

On a lozenge
Argent three escutcheons gules (Hay), impaling, Qly, 1st and 4th, Gules
three cross crosslets in bend or (Wrench), 2nd and 3rd, Ermine three

leopards passant azure (Adams)
Crests: Dexter, A goat's head erased armed or   Sinister, A demi-arm
grasping a cross crosslet or   Motto: Spare Nought
Unidentified

CASHEL Cathedral (Tipperary)

1. Sinister background black

Azure an Archiepiscopal staff in pale or surmounted by a pallium argent
edged or charged with five crosses paty sable (See of Dublin), impaling,
Gules a horse's head couped argent between three cross crosslets fitchy or
(Marsh)
Shield surmounted by a mitre
Along bottom sides of hatchment; Narcissus Marsh, Bishop of Ferns, 1683—
Archbishop of Cashel 1691—of Dublin 1694—of Armagh 1705-1714.

2. Sinister background black

Azure in sinister chief a crossier or in dexter chief a mitre argent edged or in
base two keys crossed wards upwards and outward or (See of Limerick),
impaling, Quarterly vert and or in the first quarter a falcon argent in the
fourth quarter a hawk's lure argent (Jebb)
Inscribed below shield: John Jebb
For John Jebb, Bishop of Limerick, who d. unm. 9 Dec. 1833.   (B.E.B.)

3. Sinister background black

See of Dublin, impaling, Azure a lion rampant or in chief a mullet or for
difference (Agar)
An Earl's coronet surmounted by a mitre
Inscribed on bottom of dexter edge: Charles Agar
For Most Rev. Charles Agar, Earl of Normanton, Archbishop of Cashel,
1779, and Dublin, 1801. He d. July 14 1809.   (G.E.C.)

4. Sinister background black

Gules two keys in saltire wards outwards and upwards or (See of Cashell),
impaling, Gules a lion rampant or (Price)
Inscribed on bottom of dexter edge: Arthur Price.

5. Sinister background black

Argent a cross gules between four shamrocks proper on achief azure a key
palewise or (See of Killaloe), impaling, Vert on a cross or between four
pheons or five estoiles sable (Johnson).
Unidentified.

CASHELL Cathedral, Bolton Library

1. Sinister background black

See of Cashell, impaling, Or on a chevron gules three lions couchant or (   )
Unidentified
All these hatchments are 32" square. These hatchments were painted by Robert
Wyse-Jackson, then Dean of Cashel, in the 1960s, later Bishop of Limerick.

DUBLIN St Patrick's Cathedral

There are (1956) five square heraldic panels here but they are not hatchments.

GARVAGH (Londonderry)

1. Dexter background black

Qly, 1st and 4th, Argent three Moors' heads couped proper wreathed at the temples argent and azure (Canning), 2nd, Gules three spears' heads erect in fess argent (Salmon), 3rd, Sable a goat salient argent (Marshall), impaling, Gules a chevron between three cross crosslets fitchy argent (Bonham)
Baron's coronet   Crests: A demi-lion rampant ermine holding in its paws a battle-axe proper   A demi-griffin segreant sable beaked and legged or
Motto: Ne cede malis sed contra
For George, 1st Baron Garvagh, who m. 2nd, Isabella, dau. of Henry Bonham, and d. 20 Aug 1840.   (G.E.C.)

GLASLOUGH House (Monaghan)

1. Dexter background black

Qly, 1st and 4th, Argent on a fess gules three oval buckles or in base three thistle leaves conjoined vert (Leslie), 2nd and 3rd, Qly, i & iv, Argent on a bend azure three oval buckles or (Leslie), ii & iii, Or a lion rampant gules overall a bendlet sable (Abernethy)   In pretence: Azure three crescents or each charged with an ermine spot sable (Ryder)
Crest: A griffin's head erased sable   Mantling: Gules and argent
Motto: Grip Fast
For Col. Charles Powell Leslie of Glaslough, who m. 1st, Anne, dau. of Rev. Dudley Charles Ryder and remarried. He died 15 Nov. 1831 with his second wife surviving. The background shows the second wife surviving but only displays the arms of the first wife.   (B.L.G. 1871 ed.)

KINSALE (Cork)

1. All black background

Argent a pheon gules between three boars' heads erased close sable (Reading), impaling, Gules on a fess argent two roundels gules in chief a dexter hand couped at the wrist between two castles or (Tonson)
Crest: A boar's head couped at the neck sable pierced through the head with an arrow in pale point downwards or   Mantling: (Oak leaves) Gules and argent   Motto: Memento Mori   Frame decorated with skulls crossbones and hourglasses
For Major John Reading of Saintoff, Yorks, who m. Elizabeth dau. of Henry Tonson of Spanish Island and d. 19 April 1725.   (Smith's *History of Cork*)

2. All black background

Vert a saltire engrailed argent (Hawly), impaling, Qly, 1st and 4th, Gules a chevron or between in chief two leopards' faces and in base a hunting horn argent (Scriven), 2nd and 3rd, Argent a griffin segreant sable

debruised by a fess gules (Slingsby)
Mantling: (Oak leaves) Gules and argent   Frame decorated with
winged skulls and crossbones
Instead of a motto there is an inscription as follows: 'In a vault lieth ye
Hon Col Henry Hawley, who was Lieut Gov of Kinsale 23 yrs., and
departed ys life at Charlesfort, July 17th, 1724, aged 71 years, and of
Victoria his wife, descended from ye ancient family of ye Slingesbys in
Yorkshire, who departed ys life at Charlesfort, Janry ye 7 1271, aged
70 years.'

3. All black background

Sable a fess between three dexter hands couped at the wrist argent
(Bate), impaling, Sable a bend and in sinister chief a castle argent
(Plunket)
Crest: A dexter hand couped at the wrist erect apaume or
Mantling: (Oak leaves) Gules and or   Frame decorated with skulls
crossbones and hourglasses
Instead of a motto there is an inscription as follows: 'Underneath
lyeth ye Body of ye Honble Collo George Bate, Lieut-Gov of ye Town
and Fort of Kinsale, Who Departed ys Life at ye said Fort on Monday,
ye 31st Aug, 1725 in ye 58 year of his age, and also Dame Mary
Plunket, relict of Collo Geo Bate who dyed Feb. ye 22, 1727, aged
50 years.'

4. All black background

Or three bars nebuly gules (Lovel), impaling, Sable a fess or between
three dexter hands couped at the wrist argent (Bate)
Crest: A talbot passant argent   Mantling: (Oak leaves) Gules and
argent   Instead of a motto there is an inscription as follows:
'Underneath lyes the body of CAPT GEORE LOVEL, son of SAML
LOVEL, ESQR of ye Inner Temple, Esq, son of Salathiel Lovel, Baron
of the Exchequer, Recorder of London, depart thys life March ye 24th
1748, aged 46 years; also ye body of Mrs Mary Cavendish, wife of
Jon Cavendish, Esqr, Collo of Kinsale, Daughr of ye Honble Collo
Geo Bate, Lieut-Governr of Charles Fort, and Relict of Capt Geo
Lovel; Departed This Life 8 March, 1752, in the 39th year of Her
Age.'

5. All black background

Or a chevron between three eagles displayed vert (Blewitt)
Crest: A squirrel sejant holding an acorn proper   Mantling: Gules and
argent   A skull below the inscription
Instead of a motto there is an inscription as follows: 'Near this place is
interred the body of Edward Blewitt, Esq, late of Salford, who died in
this town the 27 day of April, 1766 aged 25 years.'
(Four of the above hatchments include inscriptions which suggests that
they were used as memorial panels rather than hatchments.)

LIMERICK (Limerick)

1. Dexter background black

Qly of 6, 1st, Qly gules and or on a bend argent three lions passant sable (Pery), 2nd, Gules on a saltire argent an annulet sable (Neville), 3rd, Barry of ten argent and azure on each of six escutcheons sable, 3,2,1, a lion rampant argent (Cecil), 4th, Azure on a chief or three martlets sable (Wray), 5th, Gules a cross vair in dexter chief a ? (   ), 6th, Per chevron invected or and sable in chief three roundels sable in base a stag trippant or (Hartstonge)   In pretence: Qly, 1st and 4th, Azure a bend between six crosses formy fitchy argent (Ormsby), 2nd, Azure a chevron between three lions' heads erased or (Wyndham), 3rd, Hartstonge   Earl's coronet   Crests: Dexter, A stag's head erased proper   Sinister, A demi wildman affronté proper in the dexter hand a sword, in the sinister a battle-axe proper   Supporters: Dexter, A lion rampant ermine   Sinister, A hind proper ducally gorged and chained or   Motto: Virtute non astutia   For Edmond, 1st Earl of Limmerick, who m. Mary, dau. of Henry Ormsby and d. 7 Dec. 1844.   (G.E.C.)

2. Dexter background black

Qly of 8, 1st, Qly sable and or on a bend argent three lions passant sable (Pery), 2nd, Or three chevrons sable (   ), 3rd Sable on a saltire argent an annulet sable (for Neville), 4th, Cecil, 5th, Per pale azure and sable three fleurs-de-lis or (   ), 6th, Wray, 7th Sable a cross vair in dexter chief a ? or (   ), 8th, Hartstonge, impaling, Sable on a chevron between three heads of wheat or an annulet between two arrows sable (Villebois)   Viscount's coronet   Crests, motto and supporters: As 1.   For Edmond, styled Viscount Glentworth, grandson and heir apparent of 1st Earl of Limerick who m. Eve, dau. of Henry Villebois of Marham House, Norfolk and d. 16 Feb 1844.   (G.E.C.)

LOUGH FEA, Carrickmacross (Monaghan)

1. Dexter background black

Qly, 1st and 4th, Paly of 6 or and azure a quarter ermine (Shirley), 2nd and 3rd, Argent a fess gules in chief 3 torteaux (Devereux)   In pretence: Qly ermine and gules (Stanhope)   Crest: A Saracen's head couped proper wreathed about the temples or and azure   Mantling: Or and gules charged on dexter side with a horse-shoe or and on sinister with a Bourchier knot or   Motto: Honor Virtutis Praemium   For Evelyn John Shirley of Lough Fea, who m. Eliza only dau. and heir of Arthur Stanhope, and d. 31 Dec 1856.   (B.L.G. 1937 ed.)

2. Dexter background black

Shirley, impaling, Gules a fess in chief two pelicans vulning themselves or (Lechmere)

Crest: as 1   Mantling: Azure and argent charged on dexter side with a
horseshoe or and on sinister with a Bourchier knot or   Motto: Loyal
je suis
For Evelyn Philip Shirley, son of No. 1, who m. Mary Clara Elizabeth,
dau. of Sir Edmund Hungerford Lechmere, 2nd Bt., and d. 19 Sept. 1882
(Source, As 1)

MALAHIDE (Dublin)

1. Dexter background black

Gules a lion rampant or a bordure engrailed or ermined sable (Talbot),
impaling, Gules a chevron ermine between three seapies argent a chief
ermine a bordure or (Sayers)
Baron's coronet   Motto: Forte et fidele   Supporters: Dexter, A
talbot or   Sinister, A lion rampant gules
For Richard, 2nd Lord Talbot de Malahide, who m. Margaret dau. of
Andrew Sayers of Drogheda and d. 29 Oct 1849.   (G.E.C.)

2. Dexter background black

Talbot,   In pretence: Or a chevron between three bulls passant sable
(Rodbard)
Baron's coronet   Motto and Supporters: As 1
For James, 3rd Lord Talbot de Malahide, who m. Anne Sarah, dau. and
co-heir of Samuel Rodbard of Evercreech House, Somerset, and
d. 20 Dec 1850.   (G.E.C.)
(There is another hatchment for him at Evercreech, Somerset.)

3. Sinister background black

Talbot,   In pretence: Azure a martlet between three molets argent a
double tressure flory-counter-flory argent (Murray)
Baron's coronet   Motto: Resurgam
For Maria, wife of James, 4th Lord Talbot of Malahide, and dau. and
co-heir of Patrick Murray of Simprim, and d. 9 Aug 1873.   (G.E.C.)

WEXFORD (Wexford)

1. All black background

Argent five eagles displayed in cross sable (Colclough)
Crest: A demi-eagle displayed sable ducally gorged or   Mantling:
Gules   Motto: His calabo gentes
Possibly for John (2nd son of Vesey Colclough of Tintern Abbey,
Wexford), M.P. for co. Wexford who was killed in a duel and d. unm.
30 May 1807.   (B.L.G. 1871 ed.)
In Private Ownership

2. All black background

Argent a stag trippant gules armed and attired or (MacCarthy Mor)
The shield is surmounted by an antique crown or   Supporters: Two
angels habited purpure wings and halos or   Motto: Lamh Laidir Abu

Suspended from the shield is a scarlet ribbon bearing a Niadh Nask cross with a red insert
For The MacCarthy Mor.
This hatchment was used at the funerals of Samual Trant MacCarthy, The MacCarthy Mor, in 1927 and of his successor Thomas Donal MacCarthy, The MacCarthy Mor, in 1947.   (The Count of Clandermond)

2. All black background
Or an eagle displayed sable in chief three cinquefoils gules on a chief argent three cinquefoils gules (Davidson of Knockboy), impaling, Or a stag trippant gules unguled argent (MacCarthy, Lord of Cappagh)
No crest, mantling nor motto
For Daniel Davidson, Count of Clandermond, who m. Isabella, dau. of Daniel MacCarthy, Lord of Cappagh and d. 1877.   (The Count of Clandermond)

NEW ZEALAND
CHRISTCHURCH Masonic Temple Refectory, Gloucester St.
There was a hatchment here for a Duke of Sussex, but its current whereabouts is unknown.

UNITED STATES OF AMERICA
Connecticut
HARTFORD
Connecticut Historical Society
1. All black background
On a fess between three roses a hind between two pheons (Lord)
Crest: A demi-hind saliant   Motto: indecipherable   (Antiques, 1929)
Unidentified.

2. All black background
Azure a chevron between three mulletts or (Wyllys)
Crest: A demi-lion rampant   Mantling: Gules and argent
Inscription on back 'For Hezkiah Wyllys Esq in Hartford 1720'. This may have been painted for a member of the family or as a family hatchment because Hezekiah Wyllys died in 1741. (Antiques, Apr. 1992)

Maryland
BALTIMORE
Maryland Historical Society
1. All brown background
Argent a cross flory between four martlets sable a canton sable ermined or (Stringer), impaling, Sable a griffin segreant or ducally gorged argent

langued and armed gules (   )
Crest: A martlet sable ermined or   Mantling: Gules and argent
The fields of both arms and the background to the arms are diapered
with a floral design
Unidentified.   (Davis: Maryland Antiques Show and Sale 1987)

Massachusetts
BOSTON
New England Historical Genealogical Society

1. All black background

Sable a chevron between three bulls' heads argent/or (Bulkley)
Crest: Out of a ducal crown a bull's head   Mantling: tinctures
uncertain
Unidentified
Current location not known, probably destroyed in 1960s
(Davis; Correspondence)

2. All black background

On wood 21" by 21"
Qly, 1st and 4th, Gules a chevron between three cocks or (Gokin), 2nd
and 3rd, Sable a cross crosslet ermine (Durant), impaling, Argent on a
bend gules three molets or (Wood ?)
A label on the back reads, Funeral Hatchment from the Church of the
Manor of Ripple Court, near Dover Co. Kent, England, about 1850.
Deposited by J. Wingate Thornton 7 June 1871.
Possibly for John Gokin of Riple Court, who m. Miss Wood of
Hollingbourne. He was living in 1663.   (Davis; Visitation of Kent, 1663)
The location of this hatchment is at present unknown.

DEDHAM
Dedham Historical Society

1. All black background

On canvas 18" by 18"
Gules a chevron or between three bezants (Avery)
Crest: Two lions' paws supporting a bezant
Presented to the Dedham Historical Society by a member of the Avery
family in 1919.   (Davis)
Unidentified

SALEM
The Essex Institute

1. All black background

On canvas 3' by 3'
Ermine on a fess gules three annulets or (Barton)
Crest: A demi-bird   Motto: ... the name of Barton   Mantling: Or
and gules

(This hatchment is reputed to have been brought to Salem from Huntingdon in England in 1672 by Dr. John Barton.)
Probably for John Barton of Salem (grandson of Dr. John Barton), who died unm. 1744.   (Colonial Society of Massachusetts)

New Jersey
TRENTON
Old Barracks Museum
The Stringer Hatchment which was here is now with the Maryland Historical Society, Baltimore, Maryland.

New York
NEW YORK
The Holland Society of New York
The Society possesses a Dutch Mortuary Board which shows the arms of the widow in the centre with eight arms for the deceased's ancestors. It is not a hatchment in the British tradition.

Pennsylvania
PHILADELPHIA Christ Church
Sinister background black
On wood
Sable on a chevron engrailed between six crosses paty fitchy or three fleurs-de-lis azure (Smyth)
A cherub's head above the shield   Mantling: Gules and argent
Motto: Resurgam
Below the arms is an inscription: 'Frederick Smyth, died 9th May 1815 aged 84 Be virtuous and be happy'.
Frederick Smyth, born Great Britain, Chief Justice of New Jersey from 1765, and died 1815. His wife Margaret died 5 May 1806.   (Church Guide)
Despite the inscription, both the use of a cherub's head instead of a crest and the background suggest that this hatchment was first used for the wife, Margaret Smyth.

Rhode Island
BRISTOL St Michael's Church
1. All black background
Argent three lions' gambs couped sable (Usher)
Crest: A lion's gamb holding a wand sable   Mantling: Gules and argent
For either Rev John Usher, First Rector of St Michael's who d. 1 May 1775, aged 80 years, or his son Rev John Usher, who d. 8 July 1804 aged 82 years.   (Antiques, 1929; Church History by Delbert W. Tildesley)
See also Rhode Island Historical Society.

NEWPORT
Mayor's Office, Newport City Hall

1. All black background

Three crescents issuant as many estoiles (Saffin), impaling two coats, in chief, indecipherable a chief (for Short ?), in base, Per pale three crescents counterchanged (for Topcliff ?)
Crest: Out of a coronet an estoile   Mantling: tinctures unknown
Unidentified.
This hatchment was nicknamed the Coddington Arms from an earlier owner and is believed to have been destroyed by fire *c*.1929.
(Antiques 1929; Davis)

RHODE ISLAND HISTORICAL SOCIETY

1. All black background

On wood
Argent three lions' gambs couped and erect sable (Usher)
Crest: A lion's paw couped and erect sable holding a wand argent
Mantling: Red and tan leaves
Possibly for Lieutenant Governor John Usher of New Hampshire who died at Medford, 5 September 1726. (Antiques 1929)
NOTE   This hatchment is very similar to that at St Michael's Church, Bristol, Rhode Island, and may be for either of the parties mentioned there.

South Carolina
CHARLESTON
Church of St James Goose Creek

1. All black background

Qly, 1st and 4th, On a bend in dexter chief an annulet (   ), 2nd and 3rd, Argent six leopards faces gules (Izard)
Crest: A dolphin embowed   Mantling: Gules (?) and argent
Possibly for Ralph Izard born circa 1688, Attorney General of South Carolina and d.1743.   (Davis: Church History by Joseph Ioor Waring, 1909.)

Virginia
CHARLES CITY
Shirley Plantation

1. All black background

Per pale or and gules a lion passant argent (Hill), impaling, Azure a saltire between four garbs or (for Williams)
Crest: Out of a palisado (?) crown or a demi-lion rampant gules holding a fleur-de-lis or   Mantling: Gules and argent

For Edward Hill III of Shirley Plantation who m. Elizabeth Williams of North Wales Plantation, Hanover County, Virginia, and d. 1726.
(Shirley Plantation)

2. All black background
Qly, 1st and 4th, Hill, 2nd and 3rd, Williams
Crest and mantling: As 1
For Edward Hill IV of Shirley Plantation, son of Edward Hill III, who d. 1706, aged 16.   (Shirley Plantation)

1.   Colonial Hatchments, Howard M Chapin,   Antiques XVI, pp.300-2
        October 1929.
2.   Colonial Hatchments in America by Nora M Davis, Year Book,
        City of Charleston, S.C. 1946, pp. 182-93.
3.   Publications of the Colonial Society of Massachusetts, Vol. XXXV,
        Transactions 1942-1946, published Boston, 1951.
4.   *Heraldic embroidery in 18th century Boston*, Betty Ring, Antiques
        pp.622-31, April 1992, New York.

Chapter 8

Additions and Corrections to Volumes 1-8

All hatchments whose existence has been established after the publication of the appropriate county volume are listed below. These are recorded county by county in the same order as Volumes 1-8. Losses and movements are also recorded.

Details about identification, and differences in blazon, relating to published hatchments have been drawn to the editors' attention. The former have been included in this section, again in volume and county order. In most cases changes to the blazon have been also included. This aspect has not been considered of great importance because, since the survey started, many hatchments have been cleaned, repaired, restored, or simply moved from a dark location to a lighter one. The result is that the blazon seems different. Both editors and probably many others have stood in front of an hatchment and debated 'is it azure or sable?', 'is it argent yellowed with age or or?'. Such small corrections have only been included where they are considered significant.

Also included are details of some hatchments in private possession and others whose current whereabouts are uncertain. These have been seen at sale rooms, in magazines, and in other locations. They have been included so that the survey of surviving hatchments is as complete as possible. This group includes two for members of the Hobart family, Dukes of Buckinghamshire. These may have been part of the collection originally at Blickling, Norfolk, which has been split up. If so they must be considered with the two Hobart hatchments already recorded in the Norfolk volume.

Volume 1

Northamptonshire
STANFORD

These hatchments have been restored 1985-1991. The tinctures may be different to those as blazoned. Up to two previous repainting exercises have been removed to leave the original paintwork.

No 11 The following quarters can be identified: 16th, Spigurnal, 17th, Braose, 18th, Bruce, 24th, Hallighwell.

WELTON PLACE

Nos 2 & 3   were for sale with an antique dealer in 1987.

Warwickshire
ANSLEY

Nos 6 & 7   impale the arms of Newdigate.

BADDESLEY CLINTON

No 1   The Ferrers coat has a canton ermine

No 2   England is incorrectly painted as 'Or three lions passant guardant gules'.

MAXSTOKE

6. All black background

Gules on a chevron between three ostrich feathers argent quills or three roundels sable (Fetherston), impaling, Azure a lion rampant and a chief or (Dixie)
Crest: An antelope's head erased gules attired or   Mantling: Gules and argent   Motto: In spe salutis
For Charles Fetherston (formerly Dilke), who m. Elizabeth, dau. of Rev. Beaumont Dixie, Rector of Newton Blossomville, and d. 26 March 1832. (B.L.G. 1871 ed.)

SOLIHULL

No 4. Dexter background black
not All black background

STRATFORD-ON-AVON
No 1   The charge on the arms of Clopton is   A cross formy fitchy.

WARWICK
No 4   has no crests.

No 6 The 2nd quartering of the Saville coat is for Golcar.

YARDLEY
No 1   The sinister coat of the two coats per pale is 'Azure a wolf rampant argent' for Lewis.

Worcestershire
HANBURY Hanbury Hall
1. Dexter background black

Or on a fess azure three garbs or in chief a cross crosslet fitchy gules (Vernon), impaling, Argent a fess engrailed between three cinquefoils and a bordure sable (Foley)

Crest: A demi-woman dressed azure wreathed about the temples with wheat and holding a garb or   Mantling: Gules and argent   Motto: In coelo quies

For Thomas Taylor Vernon of Hanbury Hall who m. Jessie Anna Letitia, dau. of John Herbert Foley and d. 22 Dec 1835.   (M.I. in church)

2. All black background

Or on a fess azure three garbs or (Vernon)
Crest, mantling and motto: As 1
Probably for Thomas Bowater Vernon who d. unm. 2 Sept 1859.
(Source, as 1)

LITTLE MALVERN PRIORY
No 5   Escutcheon of pretence should be blazoned

Qly, 1st and 4th, Gules a crossmoline between four martlets or on a chief argent a boar's head couped sable (Williams), 2nd, Argent a chevron gules between three cross crosslets fitchy sable within a bordure sable bezanty (for Russell), 3rd, Argent a chevron sable between three lions rampant sable   (   )

6. All black background

Berington arms only
Crest, mantling and motto: As 1
Unidentified

SPETCHLEY Spetchley Park
1. All black background

Qly of 12, 1st, Argent on a bend gules three eagles displayed or

(Habington), 2nd, Gules a lion rampant double-queued argent (De Bosco), 3rd, Ermine a chief bendy sinister or and sable (D'Abitot), 4th, Gules a fess and in chief two molets argent (Poher), 5th, Sable five bezants in saltire and a chief or (Byfield), 6th, Sable a fess nebuly between six billets or (Domulton), 7th, Or a fess wavy between six billets sable (Dombleton), 8th, Gules a fess between six fusils or (Marescall), 9th, Gules a fess between six mascles or (Brockhampton), 10th, Gules a bend argent (Foliot), 11th, Gules three fusils in bend or (Marescall), 12th, Gules three lozenges or (Brockhampton), impaling, Qly of 24, 1st, Argent a lion passant gules between on two bars sable three bezants (2,1) and in chief three stags heads cabossed sable (Parker), 2nd, Barry nebuly gules and or (Lovel), 3rd, Azure semé-de-lis argent a lion rampant argent (Holland), 4th, Gules ten bezants 4,3,2,1 (Zouche), 5th, Gules seven mascles 3,2,1 or (Ferrers), 6th, Gules a cinquefoil ermine (Leicester), 7th, Gules a pale or (Grandmesnel), 8th, Argent a lion rampant sable crowned or a bordure azure (Burnell), 9th, Gules billetty or a fess dancetty or, 10th, Argent three bars azure over all a bend gules (Gaunt), 11th, Argent a lion rampant sable crowned or (Morley), 12th, Gules a bend fusilly or (Marshall), 13th, Azure a fess between three leopards' heads or (Beaumont), 14th, Argent on a bend gules cotised sable three pairs of wings argent (Wingfield), 15th, Quarterly gules and azure a lion rampant argent (Morgan), 16th, Argent a fess between three crescents sable (   ), 17th, Gules on a cross argent five leopards' heads (   ), 18th, Argent on a bend azure three stags' heads cabossed or a crescent sable for difference (Stanley), 19th, Or on a chief indented azure three plates or (Lathom), 20th, Gules three armed legs embowed and cojoined at the thighs or (Isle of Man), 21st, Chequy or and azure (Warren), 22nd, Barry of twelve argent and gules a lion rampant crowned or (Brandon), 23rd, Azure a cross moline or (   ), 24th, Masculy ermine and gules (   )

Crests: Dexter, A dexter arm embowed armed proper the wrist tied with a scarf argent fringed or inscribed with the words 'Hope to come' holding a spear handled or tipped argent   Sinister, Out of a ducal coronet a bear's head sable muzzled gules   In dexter corner of hatchment, A bull salient argent armed and collared gules   In sinister corner of hatchment, A talbot gules armed with spiral horns sable gorged and chained or   Mantling: Gules and argent

In base of the hatchment are the following untinctured arms Qly, 1st and 4th, qly i & iv, three lozenges in bend, ii & iii, three lozenges two and one, 2nd and 3rd, a chevron

For Thomas Habington of Hindlip, who married Mary Parker dau. of Edward, 12th Lord Morley, and d. 1647

There is another hatchment (not identical) for Thomas Habington at Lower Brockhampton House, Herefordshire.

WORCESTER City Museum

1. Dexter background black

Qly, 1st and 4th, Argent a fess gules between two greyhounds courant sable (Greswolde), 2nd and 3rd, Paly of eight embattled counter embattled argent and gules (Wigley)

Crests: Dexter, On a dexter hand clenched and couped at the wrist proper a

falcon proper belled and beaked or　　　Sinister, Issuant from flames a tiger's head argent langued gules gorged with a collar embattled counter embattled gules　　　Mantling: Or　　　Motto: In heaven he rests
For Henry Wigley of Malvern Hall, who assumed the surname of Greswolde in 1833 and m. Elizabeth dau. of William Suckling. He d.1849.　　　(B.L.G. 1886 ed.)

2. Sinister background black
Gyronny of eight sable ermined argent and ermine overall a lion rampant or gutty de sang armed and langued gules (Williams)　　　In pretence: Greswolde
A cherub's head above the shield
For Ann, dau. and co-heiress of Henry (Wigley) Greswolde, who m. Francis Edward Williams. She d. 27 June 1869.　　　(B.L.G. 1886 ed.)

Volume 2

Norfolk
AYLSHAM
No 1　The unidentified quartering of the impaled coat is for Fuller of Yarmouth.

BARNINGHAM TOWN
No 1　The ostrich supporter is holding a horseshoe in its beak.

BEESTON-NEXT-MILEHAM
No 1　The canvas is now missing.

BROOME
No 6　The arms in pretence are for D'Eye. The hatchment is for Thomas Fowle who m. Dyonisia dau. and co-heir of Thomas D'Eye of Eye and he d. before 1810.　　　(*Norfolk Standard*, Jan. 1983)

DIDLINGTON
No 2　is now missing.

ELLINGHAM
No 2　is now missing.

NORTH ELMHAM
No 1　The 4th Baron Sondes died in 1874 not 1894.

HEYDON
No 1　The crest is an elephant's head not a boar's head.

HOCKERING

No 1 The impaled arms are for Lens.
For Rev Roger Freston Howman, Rector of Hockering, who m. Rhoda,
dau. of John Lens of Norwich and d. 4 Sept 1832.   (M.I.)

HOUGHTON

No 3 Probably for Horatio, 4th Earl of Orford, who d. unm. 2 Mar
1797.

No 4 This hatchment is now missing.

HOVETON ST JOHN

Nos 1, 2 & 3 have been repainted.

HOVETON ST PETER

Nos 4 & 6 have been destroyed and replaced with small replicas.

MARLINGFORD

No 1 is still in the church.

ROCKLAND ST MARY

1. All black background
Gules a dolphin naiant argent on a chief nebuly argent three millrinds gules
(Hotblack)
Crest: On a millrind fesswise gules a dolphin naiant argent   Mantling:
Gules and argent   Motto: In coelo quies
For John Hotblack who d. 4 Mar 1895.   (*Norfolk Standard*, Jan 1983)

SLOLEY

No 1 is now in the church with two further ones.

2. Sinister background black
On an oval
Qly, 1st and 4th, Sable a chevron invected vair between three lions rampant
or each holding an escutcheon argent charged with an eagle's head erased
azure (Neville), 2nd and 3rd, Per bend indented sable and or on a chief
argent a rose gules barbed and seeded proper between two ermine spots a
bordure gules (Henderson), impaling, Argent two chevronels azure between
three oak-leaves vert (Pierson)
For Marie Louise, dau. of Charles Pierson, who m. Sir James Edmund
Henderson Neville, 2nd Bt, and d. 1980.   (Family)

3. All black background
Qly, 1st and 4th, Neville, 2nd and 3rd, Henderson, in centre point
the Badge of Ulster

Crest: An eagle displayed sable charged on the breast and either wing with a shield bearing the arms or a lion's head erased sable   Mantling: Sable and argent
For Sir James Edmund Henderson Neville, 2nd Bt, who d. 1982.   (Family)

SWANNINGTON

No 1 The 2nd and 4th quarters are identified as Notbeam and Hinkley respectively.

THORPE ST ANDREW

1. Dexter background black
Paly of six or and gules on a fess gules three roses argent (Martineau), impaling two coats, to the dexter, Gules a lion rampant and in chief a ducal coronet or (Humfrey), to the sinister, Argent a chevron gules between three martlets sable (Elwin)
Crest: On a cap of maintenance gules turned up ermine a martlet proper   Mantling: Gules and argent   Motto: In coelo quies
For Philip Meadows Martineau who m. 1st, Elizabeth Humphrey and 2nd Anne Dorothy Elwin, widow of Somers Clarke and d. 1 Jan 1829.
(*Norfolk Standard*, Jan. 1983)

TUDDENHAM EAST

1. Dexter background black
Qly, 1st and 4th, Azure two swans in pale argent between two flaunches ermine (Mellish), 2nd and 3rd, Gules a fess between three cross croslets fitchy argent (Gore)   In pretence: Gules a cross engrailed argent in first quarter an escutcheon argent charged with two bars azure a bend gules (Leigh)
Crest: A swan's head and neck erased argent ducally gorged or
Mantling: Gules and argent   Motto: Resurgam
For Very Rev. Edward Mellish, Dean of Hereford and Rector of East Tuddenham, who d. 11 Dec 1830.   (M.I; *Norfolk Standard*, Jan 1983)

EAST WINCH

The blazon given for these two hatchments is incorrect. It should read: Sable on a bend cotised or three lions passant sable (Shene)
Crest: Two laurel branches in saltire leaved proper
See *Norfolk Standard* Vol. 3, No. 6, p.86, 1983.

Suffolk
BURY ST EDMUND'S   Moyses Hall

The two hatchments here have been moved to the Guildhall at Lavenham.

KESGRAVE

No 2   is now in the church.

LAVENHAM Guildhall

The two hatchments now here were originally recorded at Bury St
Edmund's, Moyses Hall (See Vol. 2).

MELFORD Hall

The following armorial board is not an hatchment in the normal sense. It is
probably a painted achievement which was a precursor of the hatchment. It
is painted on a square board which is divided into compartments by having
a diamond shape imposed on it with a further square within this diamond.
The central shield with four smaller ones is in the central square. This has a
natural wood background. In the border between the two squares are eight
further shields; the background around each of these is painted black. (See
frontispiece.)

Central shield

Qly, 1st and 4th, Gules a chevron engrailed ermine between three griffins'
heads erased argent (Cordell), 2nd and 3rd, Azure a chevron between three
lions passant guardant or (Webb), impaling, Qly of 7, 1st, Sable a bend
argent cotised dancetty or (Clopton), 2nd, Argent three bosons (bird bolts)
gules (Boson), 3rd, Or on a fess gules three fleur-de-lis or (Lennard), 4th, Or
two bars sable within a bordure gules (Deynes ?), 5th, Gules two chevrons
within a bordure or (Tornill), 6th, Argent seme-de-lis sable a lion rampant
sable (Beaumont of Witnesham), 7th, Sable three cinquefoils and a bordure
argent (   ), The central shield has a small shield at each corner:

Top dexter, Boson   Top sinister, Boson, impaling, Beaumont

Bottom dexter, Qly, 1st and 4th, Boson, 2nd and 3rd, Beaumont, impaling,
Sable three cinquefoils and a bordure argent (   ),   Bottom sinister,
Qly, 1st and 4th, Boson, 2nd, Beaumont, 3rd, Sable three cinquefoils and a
bordure argent (   ), impaling, Tornill

The central part is surrounded by eight shields.

Top dexter, Cordell arms only,   Top centre, Qly as dexter of central coat
Esquire's helm

Crest: A cockatrice wings closed vert wattled and beaked or   Mantling:
Gules and argent

Top sinister, Cordell, impaling, Webb,   Dexter centre, Clopton, impaling,
Qly, 1st, Boson, 2nd, Lennard, 3rd, Deynes, 4th, Tornill, 5th, Beaumont, 6th,
Sable three cinquefoils and a bordure argent (   )

Sinister centre, Qly as sinister of centre coat   Bottom dexter, Qly, 1st,
Boson, 2nd, Beaumont, 3rd, Sable three cinquefoils and a bordure argent
(   ), 4th, Tornill, impaling, Lennard

Bottom centre, Qly, 1st and 4th, qly i & iv, Cordell, ii & iii, Webb, 2nd,
three coats per pale, i, Boson, ii, Deynes, iii, Tornill, 3rd, three coats per
pale, i, Boson, ii, Beaumont, iii, Sable three cinquefoils and a bordure argent
(   )   Esquire's helm

Crest: A cockatrice wings closed vert wattled and beaked or   Mantling:
Gules and argent

Bottom sinister, Qly of 5, 1st, Boson, 2nd, Beaumont, 3rd, Sable three
cinquefoils and a bordure argent (   ), 4th, Tornill, 5th, Lennard

Motto: Je n'oblierai pas

For Sir William Cordell of Melford Hall who m. Mary, dau. of Richard

Clopon by his second wife, Margaret Bozen. Sir William died 1581 and his wife died 1584.
This board was found in the basement of Holy Trinity Hospital which was founded under the terms of the will of Sir William Cordell.

WOODBRIDGE

No 1 All red background

No 3 Mantling: Gules and argent   Motto: Vivit post funera virtus

Volume 3

Durham

AUCKLAND ST HELEN

No 2 The 2nd and 3rd quarters are for Johnson. The identification is: For Sir Robert Johnson-Eden, 5th Bt., who d. unm. 14 Sept 1844. (B.P. 1875 ed.)

BRANCEPETH

No 5   is no longer missing.

DURHAM Cathedral

The hatchments recorded here have been restored and now hang in various cathedral buildings.

HARTLEPOOL

1. All black background
Argent on a chevron between three mullets sable as many escallops argent, in dexter chief the badge of Ulster (Blackett)
Crest: A hawk's head erased proper   Mantling: Gules and argent
Possibly for Sir William Blackett Bt., who d. 16 May 1680   (B.P. 1852 ed.)

HAUGHTON-LE-SKERNE

No 1 The maiden name of Elizabeth Alexander was Helmerow not Dixie. Otherwise the identification is correct.   (Surtees *History of Durham* vol. i, p.208.)

PENSHAW

1. All black background
Qly, 1st and 4th, Sable a fess between three lambs passant argent (Lambton), 2nd and 3rd, Gules three crescents ermine (Freville)
In pretence: Argent three calves passant sable (Metcalfe)
Crest: A ram's head cabossed argent   Mantling: Gules and 'brown'
Motto: Mors iter vitam
For Nicholas Lambton, who m. 2nd Elizabeth Metcalfe, and d. 17 April 1778.   (M.I. at Houghton-le-Spring)

STAINDROP

No 2   The fess of the Russell impalement is sable.

No 6   The 2nd and 3rd quarters of escutcheon of pretence are for
Atkinson.

SUNDERLAND Museum

1. All black background

Gules two bars gemel and a chief argent (Thornhill), impaling, Argent
three barrulets sable over all a lion rampant or armed argent and langued
gules (Maude)
Crest: A woman's head couped below the shoulders proper vested gules
crined and ducally crowned or issuant therefrom a hawthorn tree in
bloom proper   Mantling: Gules and argent   Skull in base
For John Thornhill, JP of Bishopwearmouth, who m. Margaret dau. of
Joseph Maude of Sunderland and d. 1802   (B.L.G. 1853 ed.)

Lancashire
CHILDWALL

No 6   In the Bamber arms the lion passant is argent.

No 9   The Bamber arms are as no 7.

No 10   For Alice, wife of Arthur Onslow, Collector of Customs, who was
bur. 27 Oct 1800.   (P.R.)

FARNWORTH

No 1   The field of the Wentworth arms is sable.

No 4   The Parker stags' heads are cabossed.

No 6   The canton of the Aston quartering is charged as Hoghton in No 7.

No 7   The label for difference applies to the whole of the dexter
impalement. Sir Henry de Hoghton's father was still living at this time.

FENISCOWLES

1. Dexter background black

Argent on a fess cotised azure between in chief two martlets sable and in
base a rose gules three lozenges or, in centre chief the badge of Ulster
(Feilden)
Crest: A nuthatch perched on a hazel branch proper   Motto:
Resurgam
For Sir William Fielden, Bt., who m. Mary Haugton, dau. of Edmund
Jackson (she d. 1867) and d. 17 May 1850.   (B.P. 1875 ed.)

2. Dexter background black

Sable a fess between three mascles argent (Whittaker), impaling, Argent on a fess sable three lozenges or (Fielden)

Crest: A horse passant argent   Motto: Resurgam

For Rev. Dr. J. W. Whittaker, Vicar of Blackburn, who m. Mary Haugton, eldest dau. of Sir William Fielden Bt., and d. 3 Aug 1854.   (B.P. 1875 ed.)

HOOLE

No 1   This can be identified as 'Probably for James Rothwell of Manor House, Much Hoole who d. 6 Oct 1824'.

POULTON-LE-FYLDE

No 4   In the 4th quarter there is no bordure and in the 5th quarter, for eagles' heads read cocks' heads.

No 5   The Winckley quartering should read 'Per pale argent and sable an eagle displayed per pale gules and argent'.

STANDISH

No 4   The crests are: An owl with a rat in its talons proper; A holly tree fully topped proper.

No 2   The crest should be blazoned as the first of the crests of No 4.

Yorkshire
BARDSEY

No 1   There is a duplicate at The Abbey Hotel, Penzance.

BARDEN

No 2   The hatchment has been moved to Bolton Abbey, Yorkshire.

BEVERLEY Minster

1. Sinister background black

Qly, 1st and 4th, Gules a chevron ermine between three broken spears erect headed argent shafts or (Pennyman), 2nd and 3rd, Or on a chevron azure a martlet between two pheons or (Warton), in dexter chief of first quarter the Badge of Ulster, impaling, Vert on a chevron between three stags trippant or three cinquefoils gules (Robinson)   Mantling: Gules and argent   Motto: Fortiter et fideliter

For Charlotte, dau. of Bethel Robinson of Calwick, who m. Sir William Henry Pennyman, 7th Bt. and d.   (B.P. 1875 ed.)

2. All black background

Arms: as 1

Crest: Out of a mural crown gules a lion's head or pierced through the neck
with a broken spear in bend head to the sinister headed argent shaft or
Mantling and motto: As 1
For Sir William Henry Pennyman, 7th Bt. of Ormesby, who d. 1852
(B.P. 1875 ed.)

3. Sinister background black

Gules a chevron between three griffins' heads erased or (Ellison), impaling,
Qly, 1st and 4th, Gules three bars or (Berry), 2nd and 3rd, Gules a chevron
ermine between three spears erect proper (Pennyman)
For Mary Pennyman, dau. of William Berry and Mary, née Pennyman, who
m. Henry Ellison and d. 25 Sept 1826.   (M.I.)

4. All black background

Gules a chevron argent between three griffins' heads erased or (Ellison),
impaling, Qly, 1st and 4th, Berry, 2nd and 3rd, (Pennyman)
Crest: A griffin's head erased argent   Mantling: Gules and argent
Motto: Resurgam
For Henry Ellison who d. 2 July 1836   (M.I.)

BOLTON Abbey

No 1 This is in the house not the Abbey. The mantling is azure and argent.
The two supporters are collared with three roses azure with centres argent
charged with a fret sable. The crest is a serpent nowed proper.

No 2 This hatchment has been moved to here from Barden (Yorskshire).

BOLTON Castle

1. Sinister background black

Two shields joined at their inner edges   Dexter, Sable three swords in pile
points downwards argent pommels and hilts or on a canton argent an
escutcheon sable charged with a salmon haurient argent (Orde-Powlett),
Sinister, Qly, 1st and 4th, Gules a fess ermine (Crawfurd), 2nd and 3rd,
Argent three escutcheons sable (Loudoun)   In pretence: Gules a fess
ermine overall two spears in saltire argent (Crawfurd of Crosby)
Baroness's Coronet
For Letitia, dau. of Col. Robert Crawfurd of Newfield, Ayrshire, who m.
William Henry, 3rd Baron Bolton, and d. 4 Jan 1882.   (G.E.C.; B.L.G.
1853 ed.)

BRANDESBURTON

1. All black background

Or on a chevron sable between three moors' heads couped proper wreathed
with roses argent three falcons' heads erased argent in centre chief a martlet
gules for difference (Blackmore)
Crest: A unicorn's head or with a scarf sable semé of roses argent
Mantling: Or, argent and sable   Motto: Sans reculer jamais
For Timothy James Blackmore, 1963-1987, who was killed in Colombia,
while working on a UK-Govt. aid programme (coffee vs cocaine),
6 Dec 1987.   (Family)

CROFT-ON-TEES

1. Dexter background black
Qly, 1st and 4th, Per bend dancetty argent and azure 3 cinquefoils, 2 in chief 1 in base, counterchanged (Chaytor), 2nd and 3rd, Sable a saltire or (Clervaux)
Creest: A stag's head erased lozengy argent and azure   Mantling: Gules and argent   Motto: Fortune le veut
Probably for William Chaytor of Croft Hall, who m. Jane Lee and d. 1819. (B.p. 1841 ed.)

CUSWORTH Hall

No 1 has been moved to Church Cottage; date of burial is 13 May 1786.

No 2 The date of burial is 3 Feb 1783.

No 5 has been moved to Cusworth Grebe.
The hatchment from Hampole is now here.

SOUTH DALTON
No 6 For 1780 read 1870.

ECCLESFIELD

No 3 is now missing.

GUISLEY

Nos 1 & 2 are in store.

Nos 3, 4, 5 & 6 have been restored.

HALE

These hatchments were lost in a fire. Reproductions have been made from colour photographs and these now hang in the church.

HAMPOLE

No 1 This hatchment is now at Cusworth Hall. The bird of the sinister crest is a stork.

HARTHILL

Nos 1 & 2 have been restored and rehung.

No 3 is now lost.

HESSLE

1. Dexter background black
Vert on a chevron between three stags trippant or in centre chief a bezant on a chief per fess gules and argent an eagle displayed counterchanged (Pease), impaling, Argent on a fess gules between three popinjays vert (Twenge)

Crest: An eagle's head erased argent   Mantling: Gules and argent
Motto: Resurgam   A skull in base
Dates on the frame '29 Mar 1807' and '22 Nov 1816'
For Joseph Robinson of Hesslewood, who assumed the name of Pease in
1773 and m. Anne dau. of Nicholas Twigge. He d. 29 Mar 1807. His
wife d. 1816 and her date of death was subsequently added.   (B.L.G.)
This hatchment was in Hesslewood House until 1985.

2. Dexter background black
Azure a hazel tree couped proper fructed or between three ducal coronets
or (Alec-Smith)   In pretence: Argent on a chevron engrailed azure
between three martlets sable winged argent three crescents or (Walker)
Crest: Out of a ducal coronet or a cubit arm proper holding a spear or
Mantling: Azure and or   Mottoes: Above, Semper paratus   Below,
Non mihi sed civitatu
For Rupert Alexander Alec-Smith who d. 23 December 1983 (Miss
Alex Alec-Smith).
The arms of Alec-Smith were granted in 1953. The arms on the
hatchment are identical to those on the monument of Mr. Alec-Smith's
parents, Alexander Smith, d. 1927 and Ada, neé Walker.

HICKLETON
Nos 3, 4, 8 & 9 Have been moved to the stable block of Hickleton
Hall.

No 11 For Sir John Jackson, who m. 1594, Elizabeth, dau. of Sir John
Savile of Methley.   (Hunter, South Yorkshire; Foster).

HUNMANBY
No 6 This hatchment could have been painted for Bertram Osbaldeston-
Mitford who m. his cousin Frances dau. of Capt Henry Mitford, R.N. and
d. 27 Feb 1842.   (B.L.G. 1937 ed.)

KIRKLEATHAM
No 1 The 2nd and 3rd quarters are for 'Pinckney'.

KIRKLEATHAM Old Hall Museum
All four hatchments from Upleatham are now here.

MARRICK Priory
No 1 This hatchment is now hanging so that both sides are visible. The
coronet is that of a Duke and not a Marquess. The hatchment can be
identified as for Charles, 5th Duke of Bolton, who d. 5 July 1765.
(B.P. 1875 ed.)

MAPPLETON

No 1 This hatchment is now identified: Qly, 1st and 4th, Brough, 2nd, for Flynton, 3rd, Mayne, impaling, Calvert
For Susanna, d. of Edward Calvert, who m. William Brough and d. 22 Jan 1822 (Poulston History of Holderness)

GREAT MITTON

No 1 The 3rd quarter of dexter coat is Heveningham.

POCKLEY

1. Dexter background black
Per chevron engrailed gules and argent three talbots' heads erased counterchanged langued azure (Duncombe), impaling, Or a fess checky argent and azure surmounted of a bend engrailed within a double tressure flory counterflory gules (Stewart)
Baron's coronet   Crest: Out of a ducal coronet a horse's hind leg sable shod argent   Mantle: Gules and ermine   Supporters: Dexter, A grey horse gutty d'or ducally gorged or,   Sinister, A lion argent seme-de-lis sable ducally crowned or issuant therefrom three feathers argent
Motto: Deo regi patriae
For William Duncombe, 2nd Baron Feversham, who m. Louisa, dau. of George, 8th Earl of Galloway. He d. 11 Feb 1867. (G.E.C.)
This hatchment was transferred from the estate office to the church *c*.1980.

RICHMOND

No 1 is now missing.

ROWLEY

1. All black background
Azure a chevron argent between three mullets or (Hildyard)
Crest: A cock sable, comb, wattles and legs gules   Mantling: Azure and or   Motto scroll but no motto
For Canon Christopher Hildyard, a minor Canon of Westminster Abbey who d.17 May 1987.
This hatchment was painted in 1992 by Thomas Richardson of Hull. (Church Warden)

SANDAL Magna

No 2 For the escutcheon of pretence read: Qly, 1st, Argent a cross patonce sable over all a bend gules (Swinnerton), 2nd, Sable a chevron between three gauntlets argent (Gunter), 3rd, Per pale gules and azure ... (for Herbert), 4th, Argent a cross patonce sable (Milbourne)

SPROTBOROUGH

No 3   The necks of the dragons in the crest are intertwined not crossed.

STANWICK

No 5   Plantagenet should read Fitz-Payn with the lions argent not or.

TEMPLE NEWSAM

No 4   The second quarter of escutcheon of pretence is unidentified.

TONG

No 6   The 15th quarter is Rochdale not Bowling.

UPLEATHAM

These hatchments are now at Kirkleatham Old Hall Museum.

No 1   The sinister arms are probably intended to represent Pennyman but should have been painted for Penn.   Anthony Lowther m. 1667 Margaret, dau. of Sir William Penn and d. before 1709.

WENTWORTH (Old Church)

These hatchments have been restored.

WESTON

No 4   The chief of Carter arms is engrailed (No 5 is not).

WHIXLEY

No 1   The Tancred arms have a fleur-de-lis argent for difference. This means the identification should now read 'unidentified'.

EAST WITTON

1. Dexter background black

Two oval shields, the dexter overlapping the sinister   Dexter, encircled by the collar and pendant therefrom the Badge of the Order of the Thistle, Qly, 1st and 4th, Or a saltire and a chief gules on a canton argent a lion rampant azure (Bruce), 2nd and 3rd, Argent a chevron gules between three caps azure (Brudenell)   Sinister, Qly, as dexter, impaling, to the dexter, Qly, 1st and 4th, Ermine on a fess sable a castle argent on a canton gules a martlet or (Hill)
(The 1st, 2nd, 3rd and part of the 4th quarter of this coat are obscured by the dexter oval), and to the sinister, Argent a fret sable (Tollemache)
Marquess's coronet   Crests: Dexter, A lion statant azure   Sinister, A seahorse naiant proper   Motto: Fuimus
Supporters: Two wild men proper, wreathed about the temples and loins

vert each holding a standard showing the arms of Bruce.
For Charles, 1st Marquis of Aylesbury, K.T., who m. 1st, Henrietta Maria, d. 1831, dau. of Noel, 1st Lord Berwick, and 2nd Maria Elizabeth dau. of Hon Charles Tollemache and d. 4 Jan 1856.   (B.P. 1875 ed.)
There is a duplicate hatchment at Great Bedwyn, Wilts.

WRAGBY, Nostell Priory

No 1   The crest is not a crest but decorative ornament. The Henshaw arms should be blazoned, Argent a chevron sable ermined argent between three heronshaws sable.

No 2   The Henshaw chevron is sable.

No 3   The Henshaw chevron is sable. The cushion of the Du Hervert arms is azure.

No 4   The cushion of the Du Hervert arms is gules.

No 5   The owl is proper and the cushion is gules. The demi-eagle of the crest is collared with a ducal coronet.

No 6   The demi-eagle of the crest is collared or.

No 7   The demi-eagle of the crest has no collar.

No 8   The demi-eagle of the crest is collared with a ducal coronet.

YORK St William's College

No 2   is confirmed to be for Queen Victoria.

Volume 4

Berkshire
CLEWER

1. The arms fill completely the diamond frame
Azure two lions passant or, in chief the Badge of Ulster (Barry)
Possibly for Sir Edward Arthur Barry, 2nd Bt. or either of his wives who both predeceased him. He d. 23 July 1949.   (B.P. 1979 ed.)

WINDSOR Cumberland Lodge, The Great Park
1. All black background
Qly of 13, 1st, Sable a fess ermine in dexter chief the badge of Ulster (Wintour), 2nd, Argent a chevron engrailled gules between three estoils

azure (Kempe), 3rd, Vert three fish fesswise in pale or (Cromelyn), 4th,
Or two lions passant azure (Somery), 5th Gules a lion rampant or
(Daubigny), 6th, Or a cross engrailed vert (   ), 7th, Azure three
garbs or (Keveloir), 8th, Azure a wolf's head erased argent (Lupus), 9th,
Argent three bars wavy azure on a bend sable three bezants (Golofre),
10th, Argent on a bend azure three cinque-foils or (for Knovill), 11th,
Argent on a bend gules three buckles or (Cassey), 12th, Argent on a bend
engrailed sable plain cotised three molets argent (Thurgrayn), 13th,
Argent a saltire gules on a bordure azure nine cinquefoils or (Hodington)
Crest: On a mural crown argent a pheasant cock or wings elevated
Mantling: Gules and argent   Motto: Omnia Desuper
For Sir George Wintour, Bt., of Hoddington, near Bromsgrove, Worcs,
who m. 1st, Lady Francis, dau. of John, Earl of Shrewsbury, 2nd, Mary,
dau. of Charles, Viscount Carrington, and 3rd, Mary dau. and co-heir of
Sir George Kempe, Bt., and d. 4 June 1658.   (B.E.B.)
This hatchment is unusual in that it quarters the arms of Sir George's
heiress wife.   This hatchment was moved from Badge Court Hall near
Bromsgrove, Worcs, to Cumberland Lodge by the 1st Lord FitzAlan of
Derwent.   Lord FitzAlan was the eventual heir of Sir George Wintour's
successors.   He was granted Cumberland Lodge as a grace and favour
residence by the crown in 1924.   (B.E.B.; Director of Studies,
Cumberland Lodge)

Buckinghamshire
BRICKHILL GREAT

1. All black background

Qly, 1st and 4th, Per chevron engrailed gules and argent three talbots'
heads erased counterchanged a chief ermine (Duncombe), 2nd, Gules
three lions rampant argent (Pauncefort), 3rd, Azure a fleur-de-lis argent
(Digby), impaling two coats per fess, in chief, Gules three narcissi
pierced argent (Lambart), in base, Argent three bay leaves slipped vert
(Foulis)
Crests: Dexter, Out of a ducal coronet a horse's leg sable, Sinister, A
lion rampant argent crowned or   Mantling: Gules and argent   Motto:
Resurgam
For Philip Duncombe Pauncefort-Duncombe, who m. 1st, Alicia (d.
1818), dau. of Richard, 7th Earl Cavan, and 2nd, Sophia (d. 1848), dau.
of Sir William Foulis Bt. of Ingleby Manor, and d. 15 March 1849.
(B.P. 1875 ed.)

2. All black background

Argent five lozenges conjoined in fess in chief three mullets pierced
sable (Bosvill ?)
Crest: A crane argent beaked and legged gules   Mantling: Gules
and argent   Motto: In coelo quies
Unidentified

Oxfordshire
BROUGHTON
These hatchments have been restored, 1984.

BURFORD   In private possession
1. Dexter background black
Gules a saltire between four garbs or in centre point the Badge of Ulster
(Reade), impaling, Azure a martlet between three molets argent (Murray)
Motto: I shall rise to the life immortal
For Louisa, dau. of David Murray, who m. Sir John Chandos Reade, 7th
Bt., of Shipton Court, Oxon., and d. 6 Feb. 1821.   (B.P. 1841 ed.)

2. Dexter background black
Qly, 1st and 4th, Argent a chevron between three ravens sable (Rice), 2nd
and 3rd, qly i & iv, Gules a lion rampant and a bordure engrailed or
(Talbot), ii & iii, Argent two chevronnels azure between three trefoils
slipped vert (De Cardonnel), impaling, Qly, 1st and 4th, Azure a chevron
ermine between three escallops argent (Townsend), 2nd and 3rd,
Quarterly gules and or a molet argent in the first quarter (Vere)
Baron's coronet   Supporters: Dexter, A griffin per fess or and argent
Sinister, A talbot argent collared flory counter-flory gules charged on the
ear with an ermine spot sable and on the shoulder with a trefoil slipped
vert   Crest: A raven sable   Motto: Secret et hardi
For George, 3rd Baron Dinevor, who m. Frances, dau. of Thomas, 1st
Viscount Sydney and d. 9 April 1852.   (B.P. 1871 ed.)

3. All black background
On an oval lozenge
Arms as 2
Supporters as 2
For Frances widow of George, 3rd Baron Dinevor.   (Source, as 2)

4. Sinister background black
Qly, 1st, Per bend sinister ermine and sable ermined argent a lion
rampant or (Trevor), 2nd, Argent a chevron between three ravens sable
(Rice), 3rd, Gules a lion rampant and a bordure engrailed or (Talbot),
4th, Argent two chevronnels azure between three trefoils slipped vert
(De Cardonnel), impaling, Qly, 1st and 4th, Quarterly France Modern and
England, 2nd, Scotland, 3rd, Ireland, over all a baton compony argent
and azure (Fitzroy)
On a mantle gules and argent   Baron's coronet
Supporters: Dexter, A wyvern proper   Sinister, A griffin per fess or
and argent   Crests: Dexter, A wyvern on a chapeau azure turned up
ermine   Sinister, A raven sable   Motto: Secret et hardi
For George, 4th Baron Dinevor, who m. Frances dau. of Lord Charles
Fitzroy, and d. 7 October 1869.   (B.P. 1871 ed.)

5. All black background

Azure a lion rampant or (   )

Crest: A lion rampant or   Mantling: Gules and argent   Motto: Intro ut exeam

Unidentified

A small hatchment 15" x 15".

6. All white background

Argent three chevronels braced sable on chief sable three molets argent (Danby), impaling, Argent a lion passant gules between two bars sable and in chief three stags heads cabossed sable, the bars charged with three bezants 2, 1 (   )

Crest: A crab or   Mantling: Gules and argent   No motto

A small hatchment 15" x 15".

7. All white background

Danby, impaling, Or a lion rampant sable (   )

Crest and Mantling as No 6   No motto.

Unidentified

A small hatchment 15" x 15".

The above hatchments are in the possession of Mr. Roger Warner, Burford, Oxon.

ROUSHAM

No 6   The 3rd quarter of the dexter coat is Upton as in the impalement.

Wiltshire
BEDWYN GREAT

There is another hatchment for No 2 at East Witton, Yorks.

BERWICK ST JOHN

The following is thought to be intended to be a hatchment. It does not follow the customary rule of blazon but is displayed in a diamond frame. On a lozenge which fills the entire frame Argent on a fess sable a mullet or in chief a mullet between two roundles sable and on a chief argent a dragon's head issuant from a ducal crown (   )

Unidentified

(It is possible that the chief is intended to represent a compartment displaying the crest)

BOX

No 1   Possibly for Rev. Samuel Box, vicar of Box who died in 1797.

Volume 5
Kent
MARGATE

No 20   The arms in pretence on the small shield to the dexter are for

Wall of Stratford and those which are impaled on the sinister are for Mann.

This hatchment is for James Cecil of Norfolk St, The Strand, London, who d. 18 Nov 1786.   (College of Arms Work Book; G.M.)

Surrey
CROWHURST

1. Sinister background black

Argent a chevron gules between three greyhounds courant sable collared or, a crescent or on the chevron for difference, impaling, Azure a chevron between three cups or (Butler)

Crest: A demi woman or holding in dexter hand a chaplet vert

Mantling: Gules and argent

For Margaret, dau. of William Butler of Northampton, who m. Nicholas Gainsford of Crowhurst and d. 19 Aug. 1691.   (M.I.)

2. All black background

Gainsford   In pretence: Butler

Crest and mantling as 1.

For Nicholas Gainsford, widower of No 1, who d. 26 Jan. 1705.   (M.I.)

HAM

Nos 1 & 2   This two hatchments relate to Lionel, 4th Earl of Dysart and his wife.   The dates of death etc are correct.   (G.E.C.)

HAMPTON COURT

Two hatchments from Kew church have been moved to the main ticket office here (November 1992). They are for George III (or IV) and William IV.

KEW

No 1   George III m. Charlotte, dau. of Charles Louis, Duke of Mecklenburg-Strezlitz.   This hatchment displays no arms for a wife nor any cypher. It could be for either George III or George IV; compare with Nos 2, 5 and 6.

Two hatchments, Nos 9 and 1 or 5, have been moved to Hampton Court.

PETERSHAM

The two hatchments below were recorded in 1953 but are missing since. They were inadvertently omitted from volume 5 which does record the surviving hatchment.

2. Dexter background black

Or on a bend sable a molet of six points between two crescents argent in sinister chief a rose gules stalked and leaved proper all within a bordure sable charged with five escallops argent, in centre chief a crescent gules for difference (Scott), impaling, Qly, 1st, Sable a lion rampant argent langued gules (Galloway), 2nd, Argent a lion rampant gules debrused by a bend sable, (Abernethy), 3rd, Per fess dancetty argent and gules (Wishart),   4th, Or a fess chequy argent and sable over all on a bend gules three birds or (Stewart)   In pretence: Argent a heart gules crowned or (Douglas)

Crest: A lady from the waist richly attired holding in the dexter hand a rose proper   Motto: Prudenter amo

For Admiral Sir George Scott, who m. Hon Caroline, dau. of Archibald, 1st Lord Douglas, and d. 21 Dec. 1841.   (B.L.G. 1937 ed; M.I.)

3. All black background

On a lozenge surmounted by a cherub's head

Qly, 1st and 4th, Gules a lion passant gardant between two roses in pale argent seeded or between two flaunches argent each charged with a lion rampant sable (Dawkins), 2nd and 3rd, Gules on a chevron between three boars' heads couped argent three trees eradicated vert (Colyear), impaling, Azure three bears' heads couped argent muzzled gules (Forbes)

Motto: In coelo quies

For Marie, dau. of General Gordon Forbes, who m. as his second wife, James Colyear-Dawkins and d. post 1865.   (Sources as 2)

Sussex
ARUNDEL

No 1   is now on display.

Volume 6

Cambridgeshire
QUY (page 4)

The names of these persons should be added to the index of the volume.

Essex
BROXTED

1. On a lozenge which completely fills the frame

Ermine a stag trippant gules attired and ungled or (McCarthy)

For Sheila Mary McCarthy, wife of Patrick McCarthy and mother of John McCarthy, former hostage in Beirut. She d. July 1989 aged 66. This hatchment was erected in the church in December 1991.

BROOMFIELD

1. Dexter background black

Argent three chevronels interlaced in base sable (Brackenbury)

Crest: A lion couchant guardant or underneath an oak tree proper

No mantling nor motto

Unidentified

CHINGFORD St Peter and St Paul

9. All black background
On a lozenge   Feast arms only
Motto: In coelo quies
Unidentified

HORHAM HALL (nr Thaxted)

2. Dexter background black
Qly, 1st and 4th, Azure between three lions' heads erased or murally crowned argent a fess dancetty ermine (Fellows), 2nd and 3rd, Argent two dolphins hurient respectant azure (Carlson), impaling, Qly, 1st and 6th, Sable a fess between three sheldrakes argent (Sheldon), 2nd, Argent on a bend between two lions rampant sable a wyvern wings expanded argent (Rudyng), 3rd, Vert on a chief argent three molets gules (Heath), 4th, Argent a chevron gules between three pineapples vert (Grove), 5th, Or a cross vair (Willington)
Crest: A lion's head erased or murally crowned argent charged with a fess dancetty ermine   Mantling: Gules and argent   Motto: Resurgam
For Robert Fellows of Shotesham Park, Norfolk, who m. 2nd, Jane Louisa, dau. of Ralph Sheldon of Weston and d 14 Apr. 1869.   (B.L.G. 1853 ed.)

3. All black background
Or a fess wavy between three escallops sable a label on a crescent for difference (Ladd/Lade), impaling, Gules on a fess argent five lozenges conjoined in fess sable between three molets pierced argent (   )
Crest: A panther's head erased guardant or   Mantling: Gules and argent   Motto: Resurgam
Unidentified

PLESHEY

No 1   This hatchment was at Langleys, Great Waltham, Essex.

RAINHAM

No 1   is now missing.

STANFORD-LE-HOPE

Nos 1 & 2   have been restored by K R Mabbitt, 1974.

THAXTED

No 1   has been restored by Christine Snell, 1990.

GREAT WALTHAM

No 1   This hatchment is now at Holy Trinity, Pleshey, Essex.

Hertfordshire
BROXBOURNE

9. All black background

Gules on a chief ermine two roundels azure (Walmsley)
Motto: Resurgam
Unidentified

BUSHEY

No 2 The arms are displayed on two oval cartouches. The Thompson
arms should be blazoned: Per fess argent and sable a fess per fess
counter-embattled between three falcons and in chief an anchor and a
bordure engrailed all counterchanged. The sinister supporter has pistols in
his waist and a sword hangs therefrom. The Raikes chevron is engrailed.

No 4 The background to the shield is dexter black, the background to
the lozenge is all black.

GREAT GADDESDEN (see page 100)

HEMEL HEMPSTEAD Westbrook Hay School

1. Dexter background black

Gules a fess chequy argent and azure in chief three fusils and in base
one fusil or (Lindsay)   In pretence: Argent a lion rampant holding in
its paw a cross paty fitchy gules on a chief wavy azure a salmon or
(McLachlan)
Crest: An ostrich proper holding in its mouth a key or with sinister claw
resting on a fusil gules   Mantling: Argent and azure   Motto:
Endure fourt
For Humphrey David Richard Pelham Lindsay, who m. Jean dau. of
Major-General James Douglas McLachlan and d. 30 Aug 1990. He was
Headmaster of Westbrook Hay School.
This hatchment was painted by Mr. Michael R W C Holmes.
It is intended that this should be transferred to the church. (See page 36.)

HERTFORD In private possession

1. All black background

Azure a fess wavy between three wells (Hodsall)
Crest: A well argent   Mantling: Gules and argent   No motto.
Unidentified.

THUNDRIDGE

2. Sinister background black

Qly, 1st and 4th, Or a bend engrailed azure cotised sable (Hanbury), 2nd
and 3rd, Vert three acorns erect and slipped or within a bordure argent
(Smith), impaling, Or chevron cotised between three demi-griffins the
two in chief respectant sable (Smith)

Mantling: Gules and or
For Caroline, dau. of Abel Smith, who m. Robert Culling Hanbury and d.
4 Oct 1863.   (B.L.G. 1937 ed.)

Middlesex
CHELSEA (Old Church)

1. All black background

Qly, 1st and 4th, Gules a lion rampant regardant or (Cadogan), 2nd and
3rd, Argent three boars' heads erased sable (   )
Earl's Coronet   Supporters, Dexter, A lion regardant or gorged with a
collar gemel flory counter-flory gules   Sinister, An eagle wings
elevated sable beaked, membered and navally crowned or gorged with a
riband argent fimbriated gules, pendant therefrom a representation of the
cross of Imperial Austrian Order of Maria Theresa
Crest: Out of a ducal coronet or a dragon's head vert langued gules
Mantling: Or and gules   Motto: Qui invidet minor est
For Gerald Oakley, 6th Earl of Cadogan, who d. 1933.   (Church guide)

2. All black background

Vert on water in base barry wavy proper a lymphad argent on a chief
gules a cannon between two millrinds or (Widgery)
Baron's coronet   Supporters,   Dexter, An owl proper   Sinister, A
widgeon proper   Crest: Rising from a rocky mount a widgeon proper
in the beak a pair of scales or   Mantling: Vert and argent   Motto:
God my guide
For John, Baron Widgery of South Molton, Lord Chief Justice, who
d. 1981.   (Church guide)

3. All black background

Checky argent and sable a fess gules (Acland)
Above the shield a lover's bow azure   At the base a crest: A man's
hand apaumé couped at the wrist in a glove lying fesswise to the sinister
there on a falcon perched all proper jessed and belled or.
For Lady Katherine Acland who d. 1966.   (Church guide)
These three hatchments were painted by Mr. Peter Spurrier, then
Portcullis Pursuivant Herald of Arms.

HAMMERSMITH, St Paul's

4. All black background

Azure a cross moline in dexter chief a key in sinister chief an anchor or
(Ward), impaling, Ermine three lions passant in pale gules (Combe)
Crest: indecipherable   Mantling: Gules and argent   Motto: Give
the thankyss th........
For William Ward, Director of the Bank of England, M.P. for the City of
London, who m. Emily, dau. of Harvey Christian Combe of Chobham
Park, Surrey and d. 1849.   (B.L.G. 1871 ed.)

5. Sinister background black
Qly, 1st and 4th, Azure four shaklebolts or (Anderson), 2nd and 3rd,
Azure an estoile or between two flaunches or ermined sable (Hubert)
In pretence: Azure a chevron between three talbots' heads or (Alexander)
No mantling   Motto: In coelo quies
For Rachel, dau. of Richard Alexander of Hammersmith, who m.
Ferdinando Anderdon and d. 4 Sept 1832.
Both these hatchments are in poor condition.

WESTMINSTER, The Abbey
No 1   There is an escutcheon of pretence over the in escutcheon of
Landell: Or a lion rampant sable over all a bendlet gules (Gibbons).

Volume 7
Cornwall
PENZANCE Abbey Hotel
1. Dexter background black
Qly, 1st and 4th, Argent a lion rampant gules within a bordure sable on
a canton azure a harp surmounted by a royal crown or (Lane), 2nd and
3rd, Argent a chevron between three foxes' heads erased gules (Fox),
impaling, Azure a chevron between three bulls' heads cabossed argent
(Buckley)
Crests: Dexter, From a ducal coronet or a demi-griffin segreant sable
Sinister, On a ducal coronet or a fox passant proper   Mantling:
Argent and azure (?)   Motto: Inconcussa virtus
For George Lane-Fox, who m. Georgiana Henrietta, dau. of Edward
Buckley of Minstead Lodge, Hants and d. Nov 1848.
There is another hatchment for George Lane-Fox at Bardsey, Yorkshire

2. Dexter background black
On a mantle gules, two crests only as the crests in No 1
Whilst this does not display any arms it is clearly intended to serve the
function of a hatchment.
Both these hatchments are small, 3ft by 3ft.

PROBUS
No 1   This hatchment is now in the parish church.

Dorset
EAST LULWORTH, Castle Chapel
No 5   The unidentified quarterings of the second grand quartering are
Shireburn quartering Bayley.

RYDER HALL Isle of Purbeck

1. All black background

Per fess argent and ermine three lions passant guardant in pale sable (Calcraft).
Crest: A greyhound courant sable charged on the shoulder with a cross crosslet or   Mantling: Gules and argent   Motto: In coelo quies
Unidentified

Gloucestershire
SNOWSHILL Manor

1. All black background

Azure three quatre-foils argent (Vincent)
Knight's Helm   Crest: Out of a ducal coronet or a bear's head argent
Mantling: Gules and argent   No Motto
Probably for Sir Thomas Vincent, Kt., of Stoke D'Abernon, who d. 1613.
(B.P. 1875 ed.)
A small hatchment 18" x 18".

2. Sinister background black

Qly, 1st and 4th, Ermine on a bend gules three escallops or between two crosses paty gules (Kilderbee), 2nd and 3rd, Ermine a cinq-foil sable (Seabroke), impaling, Azure a fess argent between three tenches argent (Wayte)
No crest, mantling nor motto
Inscribed on frame 'In God is my Trust'
Unidentified

3. All black background

Sable a chevron between three pomegranates slipped and leaved or (   ), impaling, Argent on a chevron wavy gules between three eagles displayed gules three estoiles or (Francis)
Crest: A dexter hand grasping a pomegranate   Mantling: Or
Motto: Mors Janua Vitae
Unidentified

4. All black background

Two shields accolé
Dexter within the Garter   Or two bars azure on a chief qly azure and gules in the first and fourth quarters two fleur de lys and in the second and third quarters a lion passant guardant or (Manners),   Sinister shield   Manners, impaling, Qly of six, 1st, Gules on a bend between six cross crosslets argent the Augmentation of Flodden (Howard), 2nd, Gules three lions passant guardant or a label of three points argent (Brotherton), 3rd, Chequy or and azure (Warren), 4th, Gules a lion rampant argent (Mowbray), 5th, Gules three escallops argent

(Dacre), 6th, Barry of six argent and azure three chaplets gules
(Greystock)
Duke's Coronet   Crest: On a chapeau gules and ermine a peacock in
its pride proper   Mantle: Gules and ermine   Motto: Pour y
parvenir   Supporters: Two unicorns argent armed and mained or
For John Henry, 5th Duke of Rutland, K.G., who m. 1799, Elizabeth,
dau. of Frederick, 5th Earl of Carlisle, and d. 20 Jan. 1857.   (B.P.
1949 ed.)
The hatchment of his wife is at Bottesford, Leicestershire.

5. All white background
Qly, 1st, Azure billety a lion rampant or (Nassau), 2nd, Argent a lion
rampant or (For Dietz), 3rd, Argent a fess gules (For Vianden), 4th,
Gules two lions passant guardant in pale or (For Catznellogen)
Earl's coronet   Crest: Out of a coronet composed of fleur de lys and
strawberry leaves or two single attires of a stag gules   Mantle: Gules
and argent   Motto: Speys durat aborum   Supporters: Two lions
rampant guardant or ermined sable
Possibly for William Henry, 5th Earl of Rochford, who d. unm. 3 Sept.
1830   (G.E.C.)
This is a small hatchment 18" x 18". Some of the tinctures and probably
the background seem to have become discoloured.

6. All black background
Two shields accolé
Dexter: Royal arms of William IV within the Garter
Sinister: Arms believed to represent Adelaide of Saxe-Meiningen, widow
of William IV, but with discrepancies.
This hatchment is 15" by 15" and has an incorrect background. Snowshill
Manor record this as a practice work piece by the artist.

Hampshire
BASINGSTOKE

1. All black background
Vert on a fess or three lions rampant vert (Wheeler)
Knight's helm   Crest: Out of a mural coronet or a griffin's head
erased argent langued gules   Motto: Mors multiorum vidit et urbes
Possibly for the Rev. Sir George Wheeler, who d. 1723.   (B.L.G. 1853 ed.)

BISHOP'S WALTHAM
No 1   The sixth quartering is Montagu, not Montacute.

ODIHAM
The hatchment at the Mayhill School has been restored and now hangs in
the church.

WEYHILL

3. On a quadrilinear shield occupying all the surface area
Argent a wyvern gules wings displayed and tail nowed (Drake)
(This could be interpreted as a mantle argent charged with a wyvern gules.)
Inscription on the frame 'Alexander Drake of Ramridge Esqr   A descendant of the famous Admiral Sir Francis Drake'.
For Alexander Drake of Ramridge.

Isle of Wight
RYDE

This is St Thomas' church.

Somerset
BATH (in Private possession)

1. All black background
Or three crescents sable on a canton sable a ducal coronet or (Hodges)
Crest: On a chapeau gules and ermine a crescent argent between two wings or   Mantling: Gules and argent   No motto
Unidentified
A small hatchment circa 2' by 2'.   Recorded in a Bath Solicitor's office.

EVERCREECH

No 2   The hatchment at Malahide is for the 2nd Lord Talbot de Malhide.

Volume 8

Cheshire
CHOLMONDELEY Castle

No 1   Pendant below the Garter is not the George but the badge of a Knight Grand Cross of the Royal Hanoverian Order.

CONGLETON

No 1   Qly, 1st and 4th; the charges on the chevron are not talbots' heads argent but escallops gules.
All four hatchments were restored in 1988.

SWETTENHAM

No 1   The whereabouts of this hatchment is unknown.

Derbyshire

HOPE

All brown background
Azure a double headed eagle displayed argent (   )
No crest or mantling but ornamental strapwork around the shield which is
surmounted by a cherub's face.
Motto: Mutare aut timere sperno
Possibly for William Withington, who d. 16 Dec 1833.   (M.I.)

DERBY Locko Park House

1. Dexter background black
Qly, 1st and 4th, Azure a hart trippant argent (Lowe), 2nd and 3rd,
Argent on a chief vert two mullets each charged with an annulet azure
(Drury), impaling, Argent on a bend sable three popinjays or collard
beaked and legged gules (Curzon).
Crests: Dexter, A wolf passant argent   Sinister, A greyhound courant
sable gorged with a plain collar or and charged with two mullets or
Mantling: Gules and argent   Motto: Resurgam
For William Drury Holden Lowe, who m. Hon Caroline, 4th dau. of 2nd
Baron Scarsdale, and d. 26 Feb. 1877.   (B.L.G 1937 ed.)

MELBOURNE

No 6   The flowers in the sinister half of the impaled arms should be
blazoned: A bunch of grapes between two vine leaves proper fesswise in
pale.

Leicestershire

ASHBY-DE-LA-ZOUCH

No 1   The label on the 2nd quarter is charged with a canton gules for
Clarence.

ASHBY-DE-LA-ZOUCH Museum

The museum now has care of Nos 1, 2, 3 and 4 from Willesley. Nos 1
and 3 are at the Museum. Nos 2 and 4 are in the School.

SWINFORD

No 3   Catherine, Countess Beauchamp, died 4 Nov 1874.   (G.E.C.)

WILLESLEY

Nos 1, 2, 3 & 4   are in the care of Ashby-de-la-Zouch Museum. No 5
has been returned to the family.

Lincolnshire

DENTON

Nos 3 & 4　or their duplicates, were on sale with an antique dealer in 1987.

WESTBOROUGH　(in private possession)

1. Sinister background black

Gules a chevron argent between three herons proper (Heron), impaling, Sable on a fess or between three eagles heads' couped argent three escallops gules (Wilmot)
Crest: Out of a ducal coronet or a heron's head argent　　　Mantling: Gules and argent　　　Motto: There is a blank motto scroll
For Anne, dau. of Edward Wilmot, 1st Bt., who m. 1760, Thomas Heron. Thomas Heron remarried and died 1794.　　　(B.L.G. 1875 ed.; G.E.C. Complete Baronetage.)

Nottinghamshire

The photograph for this county is for Sir Thomas Wollaston White, 3rd Bt., not the 1st Bt.

Staffordshire

ASHLEY

No 5　The Maynell arms are; Vairy azure and argent.

RUGELEY Wolseley Hall

Nos 1 & 2　are now at Shugborough Hall.

SHUGBOROUGH Hall

No 1　is still in store at the Hall.

Nos 2 & 3. The two missing from Wolseley Hall, Rugeley are now here.

4. All black background

Qly, 1st and 4th, Sable on a chevron argent between three pheons or three escallops sable (Forster), 2nd and 3rd, Vert a chevron gules between three moors' heads proper (Smith)
Crest: A stag's head erased, attired, gorged with a collar and chain or
Mantling: Gules and argent　　　Motto: In coelo quies
Unidentified.
This hatchment was formerly at Langdon church.

INDEX
Bentick Lady Henrietta should read page '152'.

Miscellaneous

The hatchments listed below have been recorded in private possession, from illustrations in publications or in sale rooms. The current location of some is not known for certain and therefore they cannot be attributed to a particular county/location.

1. All black background
Qly of 8, 1st and 8th, Azure a chevron argent between three swans' wings elevated argent beaked and legged gules, a crescent or for difference in first quarter (Woolrych), 2nd, Argent a cross moline sable within a bordure engrailed azure in dexter chief a popinjay vert (Dudmaston), 3rd, Argent a lion rampant sable a chief gules fretty or (Walton), 4th, Qly or and gules on two bars four lions passant counterchanged (Upton), 5th, Argent on a bend sable between two ravens three escallops argent (Rowley), 6th, Quarterly per fess indented or and gules (Leighton), 7th, Argent on a bend engrailed plain cotised sable three molets pierced or (Lenthall)
In pretence: Or three bendlets sable (Bentley)
Crest: An oak tree proper   Mantling: Gules and argent   Motto: A Cruce Salus
For Humphrey Cornewall Woolrych of Croxley House, who m. Elizabeth dau. and co-heiress of William Bentley, and d. 25 March 1818.
(B.L.G. 1937 ed.)
(In family's private possession)

2. Sinister background black
Argent on a fess gules between three grenades sable fired gules a roundel argent (Silvertop), impaling, Azure two bars dancetty a chief argent (Stoner)
Cherub's head above with decorative frame   No crest or motto
For Elizabeth, dau. of Lord Camoys, who m. Henry Charles Silvertop of Minsteracres and d. 24 July 1860.   (B.L.G. 1875 ed.)
This hatchment is believed to have been at Newcastle-upon-Tyne and then sold to an antique dealer.

3. All black background
Qly, 1st and 4th, Qly per fess indented gules and or (Bromley), 2nd, Argent on a chevron gules five bezants a bordure engrailed gules (Chetelton), 3rd, Argent on a fess sable between six fleurs-de-lis gules three cross crosslets or (Clifton), over all a crescent for difference
Crest: A sitting pheasant proper charged on the neck with a crescent argent   Mantling: Gules and argent   Motto: Time dominum et recede a malo

A small hatchment 18" by 18"
Probably for Sir Edward Bromley, d. 1626.
(Recorded in Ipswich in 1954)

4. Sinister background black

Sable an estoile of eight rays or between two flaunches ermine (Hobart)
In pretence: Argent on a chief sable a tau between two molets or
(Drury)
Countess's coronet   Supporters: Dexter, A stag,   Sinister, A talbot,
both proper, regardant and gorged with a collar radiant and lined or
Crest: A bull passant per pale sable and gules all bezanty in the nose a
ring or   Mantling: Or   Motto: Auctor pretiosa facit
For Mary Anne, dau. Sir Thomas Drury, Bt. who m. John, 2nd Earl of
Buckingham, and d. 30 Dec 1769.   (G.E.C.)
(Illustration in *House and Garden*, July 1991.)

The next five hatchments are in the possession of J. C. Farley's of Acton,
1993. They provide props to television and film companies.

5. Dexter background black

Qly, 1st and 4th, Qly azure and gules an imperial crown between four
lions rampant argent (Harbord), 2nd and 3rd, Argent a fleur-de-lis gules
(Morden)   In pretence: Qly, 1st and 4th, Sable a estoile or between
two flaunches ermine (Hobart), 2nd and 3rd, Argent on a chief vert a
cross tau between two molets or (Drury)
Baron's coronet   Crest: On a chapeau gules and ermine a lion
couchant argent langued gules   Mantle: Gules and ermine   Motto:
Aequanimiter   Supporters: Dexter, A lion rampant or chained and
collared flory azure   Sinister, A talbot regardant proper collared
dancetty and chained or
For William, 2nd Baron Suffield, who m. Caroline, dau. of John, 2nd
Earl of Buckinghamshire and d.s.p. 1 Aug. 1821.   (G.E.C.)
This is a duplicate of Gunton 3. (Norfolk)

6. All black background on a curvilinear lozenge

Ermine a cross raguly gules on a chief gules a lion passant argent and a
canton ermine (Lawrence)   In pretence: Qly, 1st and 4th, Azure a
chevron between three stags heads cabossed argent (   ), 2nd, Or on a
fess azure three garbs or between three pairs of crossed swords sable
(   ), 3rd, Azure a chevron between three anchors or ermined sable
(Manlove)
Unidentified

7. All black background

Qly, 1st, Lawrence, 2nd, Azure a chevron between three stags' heads
cabossed argent (   ), 3rd, Or on a fess azure three garbs or between
three pairs of crossed swords sable (   ), 4th, Manlove

Crest: Out of a mural crown gules a dexter arm proper sleaved ermine
cuffed argent holding a dagger   Mantling: Gules and argent
Motto: Fortiter gerit crucem   Winged skull in base
Unidentified

8. All black background

Barry of eight ermine and azure three annulets or (Harries)   In
pretence: Qly of 6, 1st and 6th, Vert three eagles close argent
(Smithman), 2nd, Checkey argent and sable (   ), 3rd, Argent a
chevron gules between three chapeaux gules turned up ermine (   ),
4th, Gules a talbot passant argent (Comberford), 5th, Azure a lion
rampant an orle of fleur-de-lis or (Beaumont)
Crest: A hawk argent preying on a curlew argent legs and bill gules
Mantling: Gules and argent   Motto: Veritas et Libertas
For Thomas Harries of Cruckton, Salop, who m. Barbara, dau. and heir
of John Smithman and d. 1848.   (B.L.G. 1872 ed.)

9. All black background

Qly, 1st, Harries, 2nd, Ermine on a fess sable a tripled towered castle
argent (Hill), 3rd, Azure a fess argent between three hawks belled and
collared or (Philips), 4th, Argent on a fess sable three escallops or
(Blythe)   In pretence: Gules on a chief argent three fire bombs
proper (Boycott)
Crest, mantling and motto: As 1
For Francis Harries of Cruckton, Salop, who m. 1828 Harriet, dau. and
co-heir of Thomas Boycott and d.   (Source, as 8)

The next two hatchments were sold by Heirloom and Howard.

10. Dexter background black

Qly, 1st and 4th, Argent a lion rampant vert charged on the shoulder with
three gouttes gules (Jones), 2nd and 3rd, Gules three tyrwhitts or
(Tyrwhitt), over all the Badge of Ulster, impaling, Gules a lion rampant
argent in base two spearheads or (Macnamara)
Crest: Dexter, A sun in splendour or   Sinister, A wildman wreathed at
the temples and loins with leaves and carrying a club proper
Mantling: Gules and argent   Motto: Esto sol testis me stante virebunt
For Sir Thomas John Tyrwitt-Jones, 2nd Bt., who m. 1821, Elizabeth
Walwyn, youngest dau. of John Macnamara, of Co. Clare, and d. 5 Oct.
1839.   She d. 24 June 1865.   (B.P. 1878 ed.)

11. Sinister background black

Qly of 9, 1st, Argent a lion rampant and a canton sable (Owen), 2nd,
Argent a cross floretty sable between four choughs proper on a chief
azure a boar's head erased close argent langued gules (Powell ?), 3rd,
Gules six fleurs-de-lis, three, two, one argent (Ireland), 4th, Argent on a
bend azure three oatsheaves or (Ottley), 5th, Argent a chevron gules

between three scorpions sable (Cole), 6th, Argent a chevron gules
between three roundels azure (Baskerville), 7th, Argent a cinquefoil azure
(for Mytton), 8th, Qly per fess indented or and gules (Leighton), 9th,
Sable on a chevron engrailed between six crosses formy fitchy or three
fleurs-de-lis sable each charged with an annulet argent (Smythe), impaling, Qly, 1st and 4th, Gules a lion rampant regardant or armed and
langued azure (Williams), 2nd and 3rd, Argent a fly volant between three
cinquefoils gules in chief a ducal coronet or (Madocks)
Floriated shield with a decorative urn above, a cherub's head at each side
and another below.
For Charlotte Maria, sister of John Madocks, of Glenwern, who m. 1824,
Edward Smythe Owen, of Condover (née Pemberton, but took the name
of Owen on succeeding to the Condover estates) and d.   (He died
1863.) (Burke's Commoners II: B.L.G. 1937 ed., Cholmondeley of
Condover)

12. Dexter background black

Qly, 1st and 4th, Argent a chevron sable between three buckets sable
hooped and banded or (Pemberton), 2nd and 3rd, Sable a swan argent
beaked and legged or within a bordure engrailed or (More), impaling,
Gules a lion rampant or on a chief or three laurel branches proper
(Pechell)
Crests: Dexter, A dragon's head erased proper langued gules
Sinister, From a ducal coronet or a swan's head and neck argent beaked,
collared and chained or.   Mantling: Gules and argent   Motto:
Hauri e puro
For Rev. Robert Norgrave Pemberton, who m. 1820, Caroline, youngest
daughter of Augustus Pechell, of Berkhamsted, and d. 7 Oct. 1848.
(B.L.G. 1871 ed.)

13. All black background

Qly as Dexter of 12 with no impalement
Crests, mantling and motto: As 12
Probably for Thomas Pemberton, who d. unm. 1832   (Source as
12)

14. All black background

On a decorative lozenge with a cherub's head at each side and
surrounded with the cordeliere
Pemberton arms only
Unidentified

15. Dexter background black

Per pale or and azure in dexter a tower gules in sinister on a
mount vert a sea-horse argent on a chief or three molets azure
(Garrick), impaling, Argent a buck salient gules (Viegel)
For David Garrick, who m. Eva Maria Videtti, alleged dau. of Herr

Viegel of Vienna and d. 1779 (D.N.B.)
From the Mander and Mitchenson Theatre Collection.

16. Sinister background black

Qly, 1st and 4th, Ermine on a chief sable a griffin passant argent
(Chester), 2nd and 3rd, Argent on a bend sable three molets argent
(   ), impaling, Argent a cross wavy sable in dexter chief an
eagle displayed sable (Webb)
Motto: In coelo quies
Cherub's head above the shield and skull below
For Sarah, dau. of Richard Webb of Cavenham, Suffolk, who m. Rev.
Peter Chester, Rector of Heydon, Essex. He died in 1728.   (B.L.G.
1852 ed.)
This hatchment was recorded in a Pulborough (Sussex) sale room in
December 1981.

17. All black background

Gules a chevron between three lions gambs ermine (Browne)   To
dexter of main shield, Browne, impaling, Argent two bars ... (   )
S Bl.   To sinister of main shield, Browne impaling, ... on a chief three
cross crosslets fitchy ... (   )
Crest: A lion's gamb ermine   Mantling: Gules and argent ?   Motto:
Spes mea in Deo
Unidentified
Recorded in advertisement in *Country Life*, 6 June 1974.

18. Dexter background black

Gyronny of eight or and gules on a chief ermine a leopard passant
guardant proper, impaling, Sable a bend vair between three arrow heads
or
Baron's coronet   Crest: An eagle's head erased sable
Motto: Funerals conducted   Supporters: Dexter, A lion rampant
argent   Sinister, A lion rampant gules
This hatchment was painted for advertising purposes for use by funeral
directors. It was in the possession of Messrs Henry Bottomley and
Sons., Funeral Directors, of Deptford until 1952.
It is now in private possession.

Hertfordshire

GREAT GADDESDEN

1. Dexter background black

Argent on a pile sable three griffin's heads erased argent in centre a
mullet argent for difference (Halsey), impaling, Azure a crescent between
three mullets argent a bordure indented per pale or, and chequy or and
azure charged with, in dexter chief a boar's head gules, in sinister chief a

boar's head or and in base a boar's head or (Arbuthnot)
Crest: A dexter hand proper sleeved gules cuffed argent holding a
griffin's claw erased or   Mantling: Gules and argent   Motto:
Nescit vox missa reverti
For Guy Halsey, J.P., whose father, Frederick Halsey was 3rd son of Rt.
Hon T. S. Halsey, 1st Bt. Guy Halsey m. Juliet Mary, elder dau. of Capt.
Robert Wemyss Muir Arbuthnot, and d. Nov 1990.   (M.I.)

Chapter 9

Brief History of the Survey

The national survey of Hatchments in Britain dates from 1952, when, on 29 March, a letter from Mr. Peter Summers was published in the *Manchester Guardian* requesting details of all hatchments throughout the British Isles (See Appendix 4, No 4.5 for text). Few people seemed to have known what an hatchment was and the newspaper followed up the letter with an explanatory article. The same letter was subsequently published in other national and Sunday papers, and also such journals as *Country Life*.

This was not the first occasion that hatchments had been discussed in correspondence columns. Some letters on the use of hatchments were exchanged in Notes and Queries in the 1920s. The matter was raised again in the columns of *The Sunday Times* in 1947. Finally a letter from Sir Frank Watney was published in *The Sunday Times* on 12 March 1950 requesting comments on the use of hatchments, (see Appendix 4, No 4.1). A number of people replied including Mr. Peter Summers. One may conclude that it was his response to Sir Frank's letter which led ultimately to Mr. Summers starting the national survey.

Following the publication of Mr Summers' own letters in 1952, details of the locations of hatchments throughout the country were sent to him. The numbers received over the next few years are shown in the following table:

Date		Total number reported
July	1952	378
September	1952	798
December	1952	1209
June	1953	1981
December	1953	2809
June	1954	3036
December	1954	3300
December	1957	3979
December	1960	4195
December	1962	4400
Final Total		**4850** (approx.)

A system soon developed whereby one or two people co-ordinated the activities within each county, and work proceeded in all counties in parallel. The result was the publication of the first volume in 1974. A few counties had been covered by some form of previous survey but few related specifically to hatchments. Some were a general record of heraldry in parish churches. Many counties had nothing.

Reports of hatchments came from a variety of sources and circumstances. However, requests for details about hatchments demonstrated some ignorance of what an hatchment was. One enquiry at a church elicited the response 'I don't think so, although there are jackdaws'!

Many hatchments have been lost though neglect and ignorance. The survey has increased people's appreciation of their value and has probably saved many more from destruction. Those checking hatchments have done so just in time. On one occasion some hatchments were rescued from a rubbish skip, but it was too late for the one being used for mixing cement. One family collection was destroyed because the owner was advised by an art expert that they were worthless. The expert was more accustomed to dealing with Gainsboroughs!

The recording of some hatchments has presented unusual problems, apart from climbing unsteady ladders armed with pen, paper and dusters. Those at Beverley, Yorkshire, were up a flight of 60 steps. In Scotland, Mr. Summers followed his road map towards a castle where a hatchment had been reported. He descended a hill with the castle in view, to be confronted with a river. The castle was on the opposite bank with no bridge across to it. A fisherman indicated that the nearest road crossing was 20 miles away, i.e. total journey of 40 miles. However, he advised Mr. Summers that, by starting at a particular point and walking towards a specific tree, the river could be forded. This guidance was followed carefully. The river was forded successfully (twice) and the hatchment recorded.

John Titterton became interested in the hatchments at Pangbourne, Berkshire after moving to a nearby village. He had identified two of them there and was advised to contact Peter Summers about the identity of the others. Their combined knowledge at that time could identify only four. John was invited to help with Volume 4. Subsequently he became Assistant Editor for Volumes 5 and 6 and Co-Editor for Volumes 7, 8, 9 and 10.

Information has come in from a variety of sources. In some counties the co-ordinator and helpers systematically visited every church and made a nil return where appropriate. Other hatchments were by chance glimpsed on 'Songs of Praise' or in photographs in articles on a variety of subjects. Over the period of 40 years a significant amount of correspondence has been exchanged; perhaps 10,000 letters. Whilst most of the content of these letters is heraldic, there are a few interesting side comments. In November 1973, the recording of the hatchments at Clun was almost delayed because of the prospect of petrol rationing. In June 1974 a correspondent remarked on an England-Australia cricket score of England 560 for 4!

The survey has been achieved through co-operation between many helpers. The existence of a hatchment may have been established by one person, the recording carried out by a second, the checking done by a third and the identification investigated by a fourth. The survey also encouraged a spirit of friendly rivalry. In the early stages, the counties of Kent and Suffolk were 'competing' as to which had the most hatchments. This prompted the co-ordinator of Suffolk to write a poem about the efforts of a recorder of Kent. This is reproduced in Appendix 4, No. 4.7.

Most owners and custodians were helpful and interested. However, access to record the two hatchments (now missing) at the Prime Minister's home at Chequers was at first refused. It was later granted after writing to No. 10 Downing Street, and obtaining Mr. Callaghan's approval.

There must be hatchments still to be discovered. Twenty were recorded in the first few months of 1993 for Britain. Of these, six, out of the seven which are in churches, have been painted recently (Chirk, Chelsea, Brandesburton and Broxted). The other 14 are in country or private houses. It may be significant that nine of these, and the board at Melford Hall, are all in National Trust properties. One may conclude that, although the survey of hatchments in British churches is comprehensive, there may still be hatchments to be found stored in country houses. This should not be surprising in view of the initial function of the hatchment.

The Editors will be pleased to receive details of any that have not been recorded previously. A means of issuing an update of some form, perhaps through *The Heraldry Gazette*, will be considered in the light of subsequent and continuing reports of new discoveries.

The search goes on ...

Appendix 1

Documents illustrating the use of Hatchments and other Funeral
Heraldry 1560-1818

1.1   Funeral of Sir Thomas Stanley, Lord Monteagle (1560).
          College of Arms I 13 f.30
1.2   Anne, late wife of Sir John Packington Kt. (1563).
          College of Arms I 13 f.41 v.
1.3   Funeral of Richard Burgh, Earl of St Albans (1635).
          College of Arms, Painter's Work Book 12 f.45.
1.4   Funeral of Mrs. Margaret Wiseman (*c*.1656).
          College of Arms, IB 7 f.3 v.
1.5   Details of the Heraldic Decoration of Houses according to the rank
          of decease (*c*.1660). (Ranks of Viscount, Baronet, and Gentle-
          man only extracted.)
          British Library Add Ms 38141 f.8.
1.6   The use of funeral escutcheons at the funeral of Sir Gervase Clifton
          of Clifton (1666). British Library Add Ms 38141 f.23.
1.7   Funeral of Francis Leveson Esq. (1667). British Library Add Ms
          38141 f.28
1.8   Funeral of Elizabeth, Countess of Rochester (1686) and Lord Coventry
          (1689).
          College of Arms IB.14 pp. 6 and 38.
1.9   Funeral of the Earl of Orkney (1736).
          College of Arms Painters Work Book IB 18 (1732-1742) p.83.
1.10   Funeral of Earl of Darnley (1747).
          Guildhall Library MS 5871.
1.11   Funeral of Lady Petre (1787).
          Ledgers of Thomas Sharpe, Guildhall Library, Ms 546/1 f.115.
1.12   Funeral of Mrs. Gale (1791).
          Ledgers of Thomas Sharpe, Guildhall Library, Ms 546/1 f.118.
1.13   Funeral of Lord Petre (1801).
          Ledgers of Thomas Sharpe, Guildhall Library Ms 548/2 f.91.
1.14   Funeral of Miss Rupertia Hill (1818).
          College of Arms Work Book 1813-1826, p.87.

1.1

Funeral of Sir Thomas Stanley, buried 16 September 1560

College of Arms I 13 f.30.

The paynters byll at the said funerall

Imprimis one great banner of hys armes fryngyd whys colors of whyte blewe with the Inscheecheon of his fyrst wyfe Brandone		50s.	
Item iiij bannerolls of dyscente and marryages on sarcenet wrowght with gold and sylver and sockette of buckeram frynged all his p(ar)te with whyte and blewe sylke his ii wyfes and grandmother with whyte and read and his mother with whyte and black at 26s. 8d. the peece	£5	6s.	8d.
Item a standerde of whyte and blewe sylke with the crosse of St George his woard and vj badges frynged withwhyte and blewe silke wrowght with golde and sylverceuteynynge pryce		50s.	
Item a cote of his armes with the Inschocheon of his fyrst wyfe wrowght on sarcenet with golde and sylver and lyned with buckeram		40s.	
Item 8 doossen of pencells of his armes and badges at 12d. the peece	£3	13s.	8d.
Item 8 dossen of pencells stycke at 8d. dossen		4s.	8d.
Item a helmet of steele gylte with fyne golde		20s.	
Item his crest of the Egle and Childe lykewyse gylte with fyne golde		16s.	
Item his targett lykewyse gylte		10s.	
Item a swerde with a skarberd and gurdle of black velvett the hylte pomell anc chape, buckle and pendant gylte with fyne golde		16s.	
Item a payre of mantles of blacke velvett		20s.	

Item a payre of Knopps gylte with burnysshed golde with tassells of sylke, 6 the same	**6s.**	**8d.**
Item a hatchement wrowght onto buckram with his armes helme creste and mantles and supporters with golde and sylver	**26s.**	**8d.**
Item vj badges wrowght on buckeram sett on wreathed all in golde and sylver	**8s.**	**10d.**
Item viij scocheons on buckeram in mettall at ijs vjd the peece	**20s.**	
Item iiij dossen of scocheons in mettall wroght on paper at 2s. the peec	**£4 16s.**	
Item iiij dossen of schocheons in cooler wrowght on paper at 20d. the peec	**£4**	
Item iiij great scocheons wrowght on paystborde in mettall at 10s the peec	**40s.**	
Item a wrethe of his coolers of whyte and blewe sarcenet	**3s.**	**4d.**
Item a heade peece brase of Iron for the hatchments* with a rodde for the cote of armes and a pynne of iron for the helmett	**3s.**	**4d.**
Item for paper and packthrydde to trusse and wrappe the said stuffe with all	**12s.**	**8d.**
Item for the paynters horsehyre for 14 daws at 14d. the day in rydinge downe to carrye the said stuffe	**16s.**	**4d.**
Item for his own exspence the said 14 daws after 12d. the day	**14s.**	
paye	**£15 10s.**	**8d.**

* illegible

1.2

Anne, late wife of Sir John Packington Kt.
d. 22 August 1563

College of Arms I 13 f.41 v.

From the 'Thorder of thentyrement & funerall of Anne late wife to Sir John Packington Kt. & afore that wife to Robert Fayrethwayte, Merchant Taylor of London, daughter to Henry Dacres late Sheryfe of London' (d. 22 August 1563).

The paynters Bill

Item vj Scocheons wrowght with mettall on buckeram at 2s.
the pece   **12s.**

Item iij dossen Schoocheons wrowght with mettall on paper
Royall at 16d. the pece

                                                48s.

Item ij dossen Scoocheons wrowght with cooler on paper Royall
at 12d. the pece   **24s.**

                            Sum   **£4**   **4s.**

Wheas them half were made of tharmes of her last husband Sir John Packinton and hers in pale and the other halfe of her own armes alone in a lozenge.

N.B. For alternate family relationship, see *Burke's Extinct Baronetcies*, under Packington.

1.3

Funeral of Richard Burgh, Earl of St Albans (1635)

College of Arms Painter's Work Book 12 f. 45

This parceles of woorke wear provided for the Right Honorabell the Earle of St
Albans funerall

Imprimus iij dosson and viij Taffety Eschochenes at vjs viij the pcs	14 13 04
Item Buckram Eschochenes fife dosson and tow at xxxs the dossen	07 15 00
Item xiij Dosson and vj Eschochenes on paper metell at xxiijs the dosson	16 14 00
Item one Hachment in Oyle to stand over the gatte	03 00 00
Item one Majesty Eschochen one Taffity	01 06 08
Item iiii Dosson and eight pencelles for the horces at xs the dosson	02 07 00
Item vij shafrones at iis vid the pcs	00 17 06
Item a great banner of his armes wrought in oyle and one rich taffity	05 00 00
Item a standard wrought in oyle and one rich taffity	05 00 00
Item a gydon of his bage and word wrought in oyle and on rich taffity	02 13 04
Item a coat of arms wrought in oyle and one rich taffity	02 13 04
Item ij Bannore Rowles on rich taffity and in oyle at £ii xiiis iiiid the pesse	05 06 08
Item iiij Bannon Rowles wrought in Distemper and onesarsnett at xxvis viiijd the pesse	05 06 08
Item a Crest carved and gilt in Oyle	01 00 00
Item a helmet of stell gillt with fine gaulde	01 06 08
Item a wreath of hisse colleres	00 05 00
Item mantelles of Black Vellviet	01 00 00
Item a Sword	00 10 00
Item a targat wrought in oyle and carved	01 00 00
Item a pare of gautletes	00 15 00
Item a pare of spures	00 05 00
Item iiij concellers staffes	00 01 06
Item xij conductores staffes	00 06 00
Item ix Bannerstaffes at is the pesse	00 09 00
Item x irones for the bannores at iis the pes	01 00 00
Item ij Trompet Banneres at xxs the pess	02 00 00

1.4

Funeral of Mrs. Margaret Wiseman, died *c.*1656

College of Arms IB 7 f.3 v.

Imprimis for one dosen and halfe of Buckrom escoutions	**02**	**05**	**00**
It for on dosen & half of paper in metle escoutions	**01**	**10**	**00**
It for one dozen of paper collor escotions	**00**	**14**	**00**
It for two dozen & half of Pencills	**02**	**17**	**06**
It for half a dozen larg Pencills	**00**	**15**	**00**
It for a pall of velvet	**01**	**00**	**00**
It for a hower Glas	**00**	**02**	**06**
It for a cherubins head	**00**	**02**	**06**
It for 8 bearing stave	**00**	**05**	**04**
It for a hatchment	**01**	**00**	**00**
It for 10 dozen of Bay Leaves	**00**	**10**	**00**

1.5

Details of the Heraldic Decoration of Houses according to the rank of decease

British Library Add Ms 38141 f.8 et seq

(Only the ranks of Viscount, Baronet, and Gentleman extracted).

Viscount
The rooms for the corpse of a viscount shall be hung with cloth, the corps on a haul pneu(?), escocheons of taffata for the corps a chaire with in a Travers. The great chamber to be hung with bayes with a great chair placed at the upper end thereof the outer chamber with rings of Bayes a banner 3 foot square a standard in length five yards and a half helm and crest and gauntlet and spurs sword and targe his coote of arms his circle on a cushion four bannerolls a chief mourner eight assistants to the chief mourner and four supporters to the pall.

Baronet
The room for the corps of a Baronet shall be hung with bayes and the next chamber ringed with bayes, Escucheons of Buckram a pall of velvet of 5 breadths a standard of four yards and a half in length and one penon of his paternal coat, and if he have quarterings he may have another penon of his quarterings and no more. His helme crest sword and targe and coat of Arms two supporters ofe the pall a chief Mournor and four assistants.

Gentleman
At the funeral of Interment of an Esquire or Gentleman the room for his corps shall be ringed with bayes, the Escucheons for the corps of Buckram a pall of velvett five breadths a penon of his arms, his helme and crest his coat of Arms a chief mourner and two assistants.

1.6

Funeral of Sir Gervase Clifton of Clifton, Thursday 2 August 1666

British Library Add Ms 38141 f.23 et seq

Under the provision of funeral items:

Escocheons

xx paper colour	The hall to be hanged with breadth of black bays
four paper colours	The passage into my ladies bed chamber to be hanged with a breadth of black bays
xviij paper colours	The great dyning roome where the better sort of mourners are to be, to be hanged with a breadth of bays
xij paper colours	The little dyning roome whe the ladyes and gentlemen are to be
xij paper metal	The withdrawing room to the dyning room where the close mourners are to be to be hanged with a breadth of bays
xxiiij paper metal	The chancel to be hanged with a breadth of bays
i paper metal	The pulpit and cusheon to be covered with black
iij paper metal	The communion table in like manner
one paper colour	A bredth of cotton over the church dore where the proceeding is to enter
iij paper colours	Over the street gate a bredth of bays
	Over the Hall porch a large Escucheon (called a Majestie Escocheon* upon a piece of bays)
Eight Escocheons	For the body in fine buckram

The document continues with details of hearse, rails, pall, penon, standards, etc.

*The words 'a Majestie Escocheon' have been deleted and replaced with 'an Atchievement'.

1.7

Funeral of Francis Leveson Esq., 20 September 1667

British Library Add Ms 38141 f.28

Charges for the painter on the funeral:

The achievement for the front of the house	03 00 00
The coat of Arms wrought in fine taffeta and in oil	03 00 00
The helm and crest	01 06 08
The wreath	00 03 04
The mantle of velvet	01 00 00
The penon wrought in fine taffeta and in oil	03 00 00
The staff for the penon	00 01 00
The irons to hang up the achievements	00 04 06
Eight escocheons for the body in fine Buckran and metall at 2s. 6d. a piece	01 00 00
The loane of the velvet pall	02 00 00
Two staves for the conductors	00 02 00
	14 17 06

Escocheons with quarterings in buckram and metall 5 at 2s. 6d. a peice	
Single coat impaling Venables in Buskram and 5 at 2s. 6d. a peice	01 05 00
Single coat in buckram and metal 9 at 2s. 6d. a peice	01 02 06
Coat with quarterings in paper and colours 12 at 1s. 4d. a peice	00 16 00
Single coats empaling Venables in paper and Colour 14 at 1s. 4d. a piece	00 18 08
Single coats in paper and colour 54 at is a piece	02 14 00
To Mr. Keene for his paynes in coming over and hanging up the blacks and assistance at the Funeral	01 00 00
	07 16 02

The fees to Norroy King of Arms and Rouge Dragon £20 a piece	40 00 00
The fees for their travaile at 1s. a mile a piece forward and as much backward being 130 miles from London	26 00 00
Total bill	**88 13 08**

1.8

Funerals of Elizabeth, Countess of Rochester (1686), and Lord Coventry (1689)

College of Arms IB.14 pp.6 and 38

The items listed below are those for the funerals of the Countess of Rochester and Lord Coventry. Those items for the Countess of Rochester were very similar and have been indicated in the column to the right. One notes the absence of any achievements for the lady. The only item which she had which was not also requested for Lord Coventry was a pall.

Lord Coventry	Countess of Rochester
Two Atchievements	ditto
3 doz. silk escutcheons	4 doz.*
Twelve dozen buckram Escutcheons	ditto
Twelve shields	ditto
Six Chaperons	ditto
Two dozen larg Pencills	ditto
Six dozen small Pencills	Four doz.
A Coronet	ditto
A Majestie (escutcheon)	
One great banner	
Four Banner Rolls	
A Standard	
A Coat of Arms	
Mantles, helmet & Crest & wreath	
Sword & Target Gauntlets & Spurs	
iron staves sockets	
for a man going into ye Country	

*1 doz being quartered coats.

1.9

Funeral of Rt. Hon. The Earl of Orkney
for Mrs. Marshall

College of Arms Painters Work Book IB 18, (1732-1742) p.83

February the 2nd. 1736

a standart of Great Brittain

a banner of the Order

a great banner

6 bannerowles

1 chievement 2 yds sq. inside the frame for the country

a yard and ½ d[itt]o for the town

and an ell d[itt]o for the church

18 silk escocherons) for the church

6 dozen of buckram) for the church

24 d[itt]o for the hearse

12 shield 6 starrs for shafferons

24 stars 8 banners

24 stars and garters for the pulpit

1.10

Funeral of Earl of Darnley, 1747

Account Book of Richard Carpenter undertaker,
Guildhall Library MS5871

<u>Mr. Ware Herald Painter</u>   July 31

The Standard of England	3	-	-
A Great banner	4	-	-
6 Banner Rolls	7	10	-
A Sir Coate	1	-	-
Gauntlet and Spurs	1	5	-
A Vauze for the Arch		15	-
6 Shields and Coronets		18	-
3 Do with Supporters & Coronets		15	-
2 Yard ½ attchs.	7	-	-
2 Doz silk escocheons	5	8	-
22 Doz. Buckram Do.	16	10	-
27 Doz. Crests with Do	16	4	-
22 Ells verging	5	10	-

<u>Mr. Nowell Coffin Plate maker</u>

4 pair brass water silvered	1	12	-
8 early brass coronets	1	4	-
a large one for a lid		4	-
7 doz drop brass		9	4
1 large round coronet		9	-

<u>Mr. James Wigley engraver</u>   July 29

a brass plate 12 by 16 with 10 Coats Quartered Coronet Helmet Cress Mantles Supporters Motto & Inscription waxt pollished and silvered	2	2	-

<u>Mr. Goodwin Plummer</u>   July 23

Lead for coffin, plate and soder	3	2	2

<u>Mr. Gladman</u>   July 23

Coffin Single lid		11	-
A case Do close nailed		16	-

<u>Mrs. John Loddington</u>   Aug. 1

25 plumes of white (feathers)	2	2	-

1.11

Funeral of Lady Petre

Ledgers of Thomas Sharpe, Guildhall Library, Ms 546/1 f.114v

Lady Petre was the niece and co-heiress of Edward, Duke of Norfolk (d.1777). She died 15 January 1787 at Thorndon Hall, Yorkshire, and was buried 23 January 1787 at Ingatestone, Essex. (G.E.C.)

For the funeral of the Rt. Honble Lady Petre for Mr. Lawrence, undertaker Soho

Jan. 22 1787	£	s.	d.
Herse			
30 buckram escutcheons virged & with coronets @ 16	2/-	-/	-
30 Cyphers with Coronets	1/	10/	-
6 Cyphers with Coronets for Horses Heads		6/	-
12 Shields with Coronets	1/	2/	-
8 Banners fringed and painted on both sides Coronets	1/	14/	-
24 pendants with heads	1/	4/	-
Escutcheons etc. for 4 coaches			
4 doz. Buckram	3/	4/	-
4 doz. Cyphers	2/	8/	-
4 Doz. Pendants	2/	8/	-
2 Doz. cyphers for the horses heads	1/	4/	-
12 Silk Escutcheons for the Palle with coronets	2/	8/	-
4 Silk Escutcheons for the Cushion with coronets		16/	-
Escutcheons for the church			
24 Buckram with Coronets	1/	12/	-
24 Cyphers with Coronets	1/	4/	-
12 Cyphers for Candlesticks		12/	-
3 Atchievements yd. & ½ square at £3/3/- each	9/	9/	-
Duty on primed cloth 1.6 each		4/	6
Jan 25			
6 Buckram Escutcheons		8/	-
12 Doz. Buckram Escutcheons with Coronets @ 16	9/	12/	-
14 Doz. Cyphers with Coronets @ 12	8/	8/	-
12 Silk pendants with Cyphers and Coronets			
painted on both sides large	1/	16/	-
A large Majestie Escutcheon with Supporters			
Coronets Quarterings Motto & painted on fine			
black and white felt 3 feet 9 by 3 feet	2/	5/	-
[Bill] Delvrd 8 Febry 1787			

1.12

Funeral of Mrs. Gale (1791)

Ledgers of Thomas Sharpe, Guildhall Library, Ms 546/1 f.118

Funeral of Mrs. Gale, for Mrs. Gale Executors of

February 1791	£	s.	d.
An atchievement yd. and ½ square frame and boardsMouldings of the frame Gilt etc.	5/	5/	-
12 Silk Escutcheons for the pall	3/	3/	-
12 Silk Pendants for the Featherlid Silvered & painted on both sides with Cyphers	3/	12/	-
30 Buckram Escutcheons 36 Cyphers 12 shields 8 banners 24 pendants Buckram and 2 Cyphers Do Pendants Do Banners 7/6 each Sheild 4/6 each the hearse completed	15/	-/	-/
17 Buckram 15 Cyphers 6 Shaffs 12 Pendants 4 Mourning Coaches full and completely dressed with Heraldry £5 each	20/	-/	-/
Heraldry for Church at Hackney Majesty Escucheon £3 13 6			
18 Buck 18 Cyph	7/	5/	6
Do Lancaster	7/	5/	6
Do Whitehaven	7/	5/	6
Bill dated 22 Feby	£68/	16/	6

1.13

Funeral of Lord Petre (1801)

Ledgers of Thomas Sharpe, Guildhall Library, Ms 546/1 f.91

Lord Petre was the widower of Lady Petre above. His second
wife was the sister of Bernard Edward Howard (later 12th Duke
of Norfolk). Heraldry for the funeral of Lord Petre, for Messrs.
Edwards Marsh & Tatham.

July 1801	£	s.	d.
12 Silk Escutns with Coronets and a great number of Quargs having his Lordships 4 coats and shewing his first and last wife. 1st on an Escutn of Pret. the coats of Howard, Brotherton, Warren, & Mowbray also the same 4 coats impaled for the present lady Petre 5s 6d ea	3/	6/	-
4 Do for cushion 12 Crests with Coronets for Candelsticks 1 ea		12/	-
30 B[uckra]m with Coronets and many Quargs as above described 5s 2d ea	3/	-/	-/
30 Crests Do & 6 Do for Shaffroons	1/	16/	-/
12 Shield with Silver Borders, Coronets and Quargs 2s 6d each	1/	10/	-/
8 Banners Gilt Silver'd and Painted on both sides with Silver Borders Coronets and Quargs and fring'd 6s 0d each	2/	8/	-/
Hearse 24 pendants 1s 6d each	1/	16/	-/
5 Coaches 65 Buckram 65 Crests 30 for Shaffs and 5 doz pendts	15/	15/	-/
Churches and Chapel 39 Do 39 Do for churches	5/	17/	-/

12 Silk Escutns Coronets and Quargs as before described	3/	6/	-/
12 Crests with Coronets		12/	-/
12 large Silk Pendants with Coronets as painted on both sides	2/	2/	-/
4 Silk Escutcheon as ebfore describ'd	1/	2/	-/
A large Majesty Escuctn gilt silver'd and painted on rich White Silk with arms and Quargs as above described, Supporters, Coronet, Motto etc verged with white satin	3/	13/	6/
12 doz buckram Escutns as before described	14/	8/	-/
14 Crests with Coronets		8/	8/-

Thorndon Hall

5 Doz Bm 5 Doz crests	9/	-/	-/
3 doz large silk pendants as before described	6/	6/	-/

Statehouse

4 Buckram escutcheons and 4 crests		12/-	
3 yd and ½ achievement with supprs, coronets, Mantles, and frames and Bds moulding gilt the 5s each 3/18/6	11/	15/	6/
Extra having an greate number of quargs as described in the escutcheons 7/6 eacj	1/	2/	6/
To a great banner of the arms and all the Quargs as before describ'd gilt silver'd and painted on both sides on rich silk 6 feet square and fringed and 4 bannerols contain the several quargs gilt silvered and painted on both sides on rich silk 3 feet square and fringed socketing poles blocks etc	20/	-/	-/

1.14

Miss Hill (1818)

College of Arms Work Book 1813-1826 p. 87

Arms: Gules two bars ermine in chief a lion passant argent
Miss Rupertia Hill

1 Ell Acht
2 ditto with frames for church
24 Buckram Esctns for church
24 Cyphers for church
1 Satin Majest Esctn
12 Pall Esctns
12 Silk Pendants
36 Buckram for Room
36 Cyphers for Room
30 Buckram Hearse
36 Cyphers Hears
12 Shields Hearse
8 (?) Banners painted both sides
24 Pendants
18 Eschon for Coaches

Appendix 2

Undertakers who engaged Thomas Sharpe, Hatchment Painter

The list below includes only those who requested the production of hatchments for six or more funerals.

Period	Company Name	Company Address	Company Business	Number Painted
1776-1800	Ayscough	No 1 Fore St.* Cripplegate	Undertaker*	83
1802/1802	Ayscough, Wood & Holmes	No 1 Fore St.* Cripplegate	Undertakers	13
1819-1825	Ayscough & Sadler	No 1 Fore St.* Cripplegate	Undertakers	12
1786-1802	Bacon	London, Clerkenwell	Undertaker	19
1822-1826	Birch	London, Knightsbridge	Undertaker	7
1785-1825	Blake	Fleet Market	Undertaker	30
1820-1826	Blaxland	Broad St.	Upholsterer*	11
1780-1802	Bourdillon		Hatter/Grocer* to his Majesty	8
1777-1790	Brettell			10
1777-1790	Butler/Parsons	17 Fleet Market*	Undertaker	63
1794-1822	Butler	17 Fleet Market*	Undertaker	62
1787-1797	Chapman	Coleman St.	Auctioneer & Upholders	13
1795-1802	Clerkson & Knight	Kingston		19
1785-1820	Cressal	Whitechapel	Undertaker	35
1821-1826	Cressall and Bradley			17
1788-1792	Cresswell	95 Whitechapel*	Coffin Plate Maker*	6
1820-1822	Dunn	Kent St. Borough	Coffin maker & Undertaker*	25
1776-1797	Edmundson J.			18
1794-1798	Edward, Marsh & Bailey		Upholsterers	9
1798-1802	Edward, Marsh & Tatham		Upholsterers	13
1786-1802	Godfrey	Westminster	Undertaker	17
1787-1802	Hamilton	Whitechapel	Undertaker	31
1792-1803	Henniker	Bank Coffeehouse	Merchant	6

Date	Name	Address	Occupation	No.
1783-1802	Kay			41
1785-1793	Lawrence	29 Church St., Soho*	Undertaker*	21
1776-1795	Micklem & Deane	Reading, Berks		21
1797-1826	Norris, John	Holburn	Upholsterer	15
1781-1826	Page	King St., Bloomsbury	Undertaker & Coffin Maker	49
1776-1802	Paterson, Geo	? 145 Bishopsgate St.	? Painter to Prince of Wales*	72
1780-1800	Rathell	Great Ormonde St., Queens Square	Upholder*	11
1785-1795	Riley, Mrs.	71 Long Acre	Upholder & Auctioneer	7
1784-1802	Robins	Chancery Lane	Upholder*	16
1802-1823	Robins	Regent St.		23
1782-1823	Rutt	Fenchurch St.	Glovers*	40
1824-1826	Rutt & Howard	165 Fenchurch St.	Glovers*	5
1780-1802	Sammes	53 Russell St.*	Upholder*	23
1786-1797	Scott, Thomas	Ludgate Hill	Upholder	10
1786-1799	Seddon, Thomas	Dover St., Piccadily	Cabinet Maker*	6
1798-1820	Seddon, Thomas & George	150 Aldersgate*	Cabinet & Upholsterers*	13
1819-1825	Shrubsole	Kingston		22
1792-1802	Simms, William	Holburn	Upholder*	12
1798-1802	Smith and Walbank	4 John St., Oxford St.*	Undertakers*	20
	see also Walbank and Smith			
1790-1798	Stewart, Geo	Upper Harley St.		12
1784-1790	Thornton	86 Blackman St. Southwick	Coffin Plate Maker*	47
1790-1826	Thornton	174 High St., Southwark		133
1777-1789	Towers			14
1775-1784	Walbank			9
1784	Walbank and Milward			2
1795-1797	Walbank and Smith			15
	See also Smith and Walbank			
1786-1789	Walbank, Smith & Turner			5
1784-1796	Worsley			23

These details are from Thomas Sharpe's ledgers, Guildhall MS 546/1 and 546/2. One should note that the ledgers only cover the periods 1774-1804 and 1819-1826. The occupations and addresses marked * have been added from London Directories of the period. The date span relates to the painting of hatchments only. One cannot assume that, where the information has been taken from directories, the company occupied the given premises for the whole of that period nor that the person held the same occupation for that period.

Appendix 3

Surviving Hatchments known to have been painted by Thomas Sharpe

Vol.	County	Place	No.	Name	Date
1	Northamptonshire	Brockhall	1	Thomas Lee Thornton	1790
1	Northamptonshire	Canons Ashby	5	Elizabeth Dryden	1791
1	Northamptonshire	Easton Maudit	2	Hester (Yelverton), Duchess of Sussex	1777
1	Northamptonshire	Upton	4	Lady Elizabeth Samwell	1789
1	Warwickshire	Honington	2	Elizabeth Townsend	1821
1	Warwickshire	Honington	3	Gore Townsend	1826
1	Warwickshire	Stoneleigh	2	Edward, 5th Baron Leigh	1786
1	Worcestershire	Besford	1	Sir John Sebright, 6th Bt.	1794
2	Norfolk	Earsham	2	Louisa Dalling	1824
2	Norfolk	Felbrigg	2	Cecelia Windham	1824
2	Norfolk	Houghton	3-4	Horatio (Walpole), 3rd Earl of Orford	1797
2	Norfolk	Wickmere	1	Horatio, 3rd Earl Orford	1797
2	Suffolk	Hawstead	1	Lucy Metcalfe	1793
2	Suffolk	Huntingfield	1	Sir Joshua Vanneck, 1st Bt.	1777
2	Suffolk	Huntingfield	2	Sir Gerard Vanneck, 2nd Bt.	1791
2	Suffolk	Redgrave	10	Adm. George Wilson	1826
2	Suffolk	Southwold	1	John Robinson	1802
2	Suffolk	Thornham Magna	3	Sir John Major, 1st Bt.	1781
2	Suffolk	Thornham Magna	5	Emily, Baroness Henniker	1821
3	Durham	Brancepeth	2	Matthew Russell	1822
3	Northumberland	Hexham	3	Rev. Robert Clarke	1824
3	Northumberland	St-Oswald-at-Lee	3	Rev Robert Clarke	1824
3	Yorkshire	Burton Agnes	1	Sir Griffith Boynton, 6th Bt.	1778
3	Yorkshire	South Dalton	1	Sir Charles Hotham-Thompson	1794
3	Yorkshire	South Dalton	2	Rt. Rev. Sir Charles Hotham, 9th Bt., Bishop of Clogher	1795
4	Bedfordshire	Milton Bryan	1	Catherine Inglis	1792
4	Bedfordshire	Milton Bryan	2	Sir Hugh Inglis	1820
4	Bedfordshire	Old Warden	2	Frances, Baroness Ongley	1799
4	Berkshire	Pangbourne	4	John Breedon	1776
4	Berkshire	Pangbourne	6	John Breedon	1783
4	Buckinghamshire	Chenies	5	Lady Georgiana Russell	1801
4	Buckinghamshire	Chesham	9	Coulson Skottowe	1784
4	Buckinghamshire	Chesham	10	Anne Skottowe	1784
4	Buckinghamshire	Langley Marish	2	Maurice Swabey	1826
4	Buckinghamshire	Stoke Poges	8	Julianna Penn	1801

Vol.	County	Place	No.	Name	Dat
4	Oxfordshire	Culham	1-2	John Phillips	182
4	Oxfordshire	Kirtlington	6	Lady Mary Dashwood	179
5	Kent	Chevening	3	Philip, 2nd Earl Stanhope	178
5	Kent	Maidstone, Museum	6	Lady Catherine Twisden	181
5	Kent	Margate	20	James Cecil	178
5	Kent	Otford	4	Patience Polhill	180
5	Kent	St Paul's Cray, St Paulinus	3	James Chapman	182
5	Kent	St Paul's Cray, St Paulinus	4	Jane Chapman	182
5	Kent	Sutton-at-Hone	4	John Mumford	182
5	Kent	Sutton-at-Hone	6	William Mumford	182
5	Surrey	Bermondsey	2	Elisabeth Gaitskell	182
5	Surrey	Merton	3	Lady Anne Burnett	180
5	Surrey	Morden	1	Elisabeth Ridge	182
5	Surrey	Morden	2	George Ridge	182
5	Surrey	Morden	6	William Hoare	181
5	Sussex	Kirdford	1	Edward 1st Earl Winterton	178
6	Essex	Bobbingworth	4	Frederica Cure	182
6	Essex	Boreham	4	Lady Sarah Tyrell	182
6	Essex	Chigwell	9	Wilhamina Hatch	182
6	Essex	Little Illford	3	Wilhamina Hatch	182
6	Essex	Lambourne	5	Rev. Edward Lockwood	180
6	Essex	Orsett	2	Elizabeth Baker	179
6	Essex	Sutton	1	John White	179
6	Essex	Theydon Mount	6	Sir Edward Smyth, 3rd Bt.	178
6	Essex	Waltham Abbey	4	Thomas Leverton	182
6	Essex	Waltham Abbey	6	Sir William Wake, 8th Bt.	178
6	Huntingdonshire	Kimbolton	5	George, 4th Duke of Manchester	178
6	Hertfordshire	East Barnet	2	Arabella Trevor	178
6	Hertfordshire	Flamstead	1	Sir John Sebright, 6th Bt.	179
6	Hertfordshire	Hitchin	1	Robert Hinde	178
6	Hertfordshire	Hitchin	2	Mary Hinde	181
6	Hertfordshire	Ridge	2	Elizabeth Hearne	182
7	Gloucestershire	Adlestrop	2	James Leigh	182
7	Gloucestershire	Oddington	1&2	Sir John Reade	178
7	Hampshire	Heckfield	6	Lt-Gen. Sir William Pitt	181
7	Somerset	Goathurst	3	Lady Anne Tynte	179
7	Somerset	Nailsea Court	1	Gen. James Adeane	180
8	Derbyshire	Renishaw Hall	1	Mary Sitwell	179
8	Derbyshire	Renishaw Hall	2	Francis Hurt Sitwell	179
8	Derbyshire	Renishaw Hall	5	Lady Mary Wake	179
8	Leicestershire	Bottesford	2	John 3rd Duke of Rutland	177
8	Leicestershire	Bottesford	3	Charles, 4th Duke of Rutland	178
8	Lincolnshire	Lincoln, Redbourne	2	(now Lincoln, Usher Art Gallery), William 8th Duke of St Albans	182
8	Nottinghamshire	Gedling	1	Anne, Countess of Chesterfield	179
9	Monmouth	Lower machen	6	John Morgan	179
9	Shropshire	Nash	3	Thomas Lowe	179
10	Stray	Private possession	19	David Garrick	177

Appendix 4

Relevant letters and other papers of the 1950s

The following are the texts of letters and other documents which have relevance to the use of hatchments in the 20th century and to the history of the Survey.

4.1 Letter from Sir Frank Watney published in *The Sunday Times* in 1950.

4.2 Reply to No. 1 by T. C. D. Hassall Esq.

4.3 Reply to No. 1 by Sir Picton Bagge

4.4 Reply to No. 1 by Peter Summers

4.5 Letter by Peter Summers to *Manchester Guardian*, Saturday 29 March 1952

4.6 Paper written by Mr. H. Stanford London, F.S.A., *Norfolk Herald Extraordinary*, sent to Peter Spokes in 1951 on hatchments with impalements of arms of office or dignity

4.7 'The Bromley Boy'; a poem by Henry Hawes

4.1

Sunday Times, 12 March 1950

Sir,

Recently I went to the funeral of my old friend the squire of Nazeing and head of the family of Palmer. When I went to the house I saw over the front door a hatchment bearing the family's coat of arms. Few of my acquaintances seem to have heard of a hatchment, yet readers of 'Vanity Fair' must remember the hatchments which Becky saw in Great Gaunt Street when she paid her first visit to Sir Pitt Crowley, and also the hatchment which she saw some years later over the great entrance at Queens Crowley. I have a recollection of my father showing me one over a door in—I think—Berkeley Square—in the late seventies or early eighties.

There are two good specimens in the chancel of a little church in Surrey, one of which was placed over the door of the moated house when my great-great-grandfather died some 130 years ago. It was returned to the church and has never been used since. There must be many in existence, and I shall be interested if any of your readers can tell me if in these days they are ever used either in the country or in London for the purpose for which they were intended.

FRANK D. WATNEY
Travellers Club

4.2

Reply to 4.1 by T. C. D. Hassall Esq., 12 March 1950

Dear Sir

I was much interested in your letter in today's Sunday Times re 'Hatchments'.

In 1931, when my Uncle R. H. Price-Dent died at my Mother's family home at Hallaton manor in Leicestershire, I acted as administrator of the Estate.

The family hatchment was in the parish church, and was in a most dilapidated condition. I had it taken down, repaired and put into a suitable frame with glass in front of it.

It was then placed over the centre of the main porch at the Manor for a fortnight, when it was returned for safe custody to the Church, where it still remains. I saw it there last year.

Yours faithfully
T. C. D. Hassall (Esq.)

N.B.   The recorded hatchment at Hallaton church is for a Thwaites-Dent Marriage.]

4.3

Reply to 4.1 by Sir Picton Bagge, 15 March 1950

Dear Sir Frank Watney,

In the last paragraph of your letter in the 'Sunday Times' o
March 12th about *Hatchments* you ask if they are ever used for the
purpose for which they were intended. I am therefore writing to le
you know that my family has two hatchments, one for the head o
the family and one for his wife (or widow). On their deaths the
appropriate hatchment is placed over the outside door of the Soutl
porch, where the coffin lies on the night before the funeral. They
have been in the family beyond the memory of anyone living. In
my lifetime they have been used on the death of my father (1916)
of my mother (1918), and my elder brother (1939). The coats o
arms are painted on canvas and mounted on wood.

Believe me,
Yours sincerely
Picton Bagge

4.4

Reply to 4.1 by Peter Summers, 12 March 1950

Dear Sir,

Hatchments

I was very interested in your letter in the 'Sunday Times' this morning. I am not by any means an expert on Heraldry but I think the position regarding hatchments is this. They were used extensively in the 17th and 18th centuries, less so in the last century and only very rarely in the present century. I am not sure but I do not think it was ever intended that the hatchment once used should ever be used again. It would in fact be only on a few occasions that it would be possible for the hatchment to be used twice. The hatchment of a married man, a married woman, a widower and widow all differed slightly, but in each case they bore the arms of both husband and wife, side by side in the same shield, as is called in heraldry 'impaled'. It would therefore be possible for the hatchment to be used again only by a bachelor or spinster, or by one of the family who had married into the same family as one of his ancestors. Because of this, and because I can find no reference in my books on Heraldry to a hatchment being used twice, I think it is unlikely that hatchments were intended to be used more than once. I think they were individual and once having been consigned to the Church were intended to stay there.

I have only once seen a hatchment in use, and that was hanging over the main entrance at Wardour Castle, on the death of Lord Arundel of Wardour, sometime during the last war, I don't remember the year, probably between 1940 and 1943.

If you should get any information which contradicts anything I have said, and if you can spare the time to write, I should be most interested. I should also be interested to know how many instances of recent date of the use of hatchments are reported to you. However I expect you will have many letters and so I shall not expect a prompt reply.

Yours truly

P. G. Summers

4.5

Letter from Peter Summers to the
Manchester Guardian, Saturday 29 March 1950

To the Editor of the Manchester Guardian

Sir—An important source of genealogical material, at present almost totally neglected, is the armorial funeral hatchment of which several thousand are still to be found in churches throughout Britain. Dating mainly from the eighteenth and nineteenth centuries, these hatchments have received scant attention from the antiquary and archaeologist. Many have been destroyed and others relegated to the stokehole or belfry.

The Bath Heraldic Society hopes to make as complete a record as possible of these hatchments, indexed under both places and families. I shall be most grateful for the cooperation of your readers in sending notes of any hatchments in their district. Expert knowledge is not essential. Ideally the full blazon is required, but even the bare notification of the existence of hatchments is most welcome.

Yours &
P. G. Summers
Hon Sec.
Bath Heraldic Society

4.6

Paper written by Mr. H. Stanford London, F.S.A., *Norfolk Herald Extraordinary*

Sent to Peter Spokes in 1951 on 'Hatchments with impalements of arms of office or dignity'.

No doubt there are precedents for the use of a parti-coloured background on hatchments impaling arms of office or dignity but these stem from a misconception of the nature of such arms. Hatchments (as the word is now used) are essentially modern. The earliest of which I have heard dates from the 1640's and the great majority are of the 18th or even 19th century. Heraldic science in those days was at a low ebb and aetiological myths were rampant. Among these must certainly be counted the notion that prelates impaled the arms of their see to show that they were wedded to the church. It is true that I gave that explanation in 'Arms of Office', but the more I consider it the more certain I am that it is sheer bunkum. The earliest known examples of arms of office are of two kinds; on the one hand are the crowns of kings of arms, on the other are the archiepiscopal cross and pallium. Of these the crowns seem to be the earlier for they are impaled on the seal of Guiot, king of Champagne in 1355, whereas the first English prelate to impale his official insignia on his seal was Archbishop Arundel, 1397-1414. (Episcopal arms appear on some earlier seals but not impaled).

No one has suggested or is likely to suggest that a king of arms impaled the crowns because he was wedded to his office. Still less plausible would it be to suggest that the merchant or master-craftsman was wedded to his guild and yet from the 15th, if not from the 14th century onwards examples of guild arms joined, by impalement or otherwise, in the same shield with the personal arms or the mark of the guildsman are common. Furthermore although impalement is the usual way at least in England of marshalling arms of office or dignity it is far from universal. Continental prelates often marshalled the arms of their offices in other ways (there are many examples in Woodward's Ecclesiastical Heraldry); English prelates also though less frequently—to cite but one example, on the monument in Rochester Cathedral of Bishop John Lowe, died 1467, his personal arms are displayed with the arms of the see on a canton.

If none but prelates had been concerned, this use of the arms of the see or dignity might perhaps have been compared to the territorial use of some feudal arms but no such explanation is admissible for the heralds' crowns, nor for guild arms, nor for the many other arms of office which have since come into use. In fact arms of office and dignity seem to form a class by themselves with their own character and uses. When the arms of an office or dignity are marshalled in one shield with those of the officer the former are in the nature of an augmentation and the whole shield must be regarded as that of the officer and not of the office. There is no logical resemblance between the union on the one hand of the arms of an office and its incumbent and on the other hand of those of a man and his wife, nor is there any reason why rules and customs which may be appropriate for a man and wife should be applied in the case of an officer and his office. When the impaled arms of a man and his wife are painted on a hatchment everyone knows that the are the arms of two different individuals both of whom are mortal and the modern parti-coloured background was invented for the purpose of showing that to show that one of those individuals was still living. In the other case there is no need to say that. The office is as it were immortal and it needs no white background to show that the office lives on though its incumbent is dead. That however is really beside the point for the dexter coat in such cases is not to be considered as the arms of a separate individual but as an honorary augmentation employed by the wearer of the sinister coat during his tenure of the office in question. The whole shield is the shield of the defunct and it is only logical that the whole background of the hatchment should be painted black.

4.7

The Bromley Boy

These verses were written in the 1950s by Harold Hawes who was recording the Suffolk hatchments. At that time Suffolk led the field with the number of hatchments, but was being challenged by Kent. One of the Kent recorders was a boy who lived in Bromley, and who was also a pupil at Kingswood School where I was Bursar.

PETER SUMMERS

The Maid of Kent with horrid joy
Beguiles by stealth the Bromley Boy.
The Innocent at her behest
Sets off upon his hatchment Quest.
With nods and becks and wreathed smiles
She tempts the Boy to stray for miles
To garner with an eager hand
the hatchments scattered thro' her land.

She hopes false trollop to cast down
And wrest from Suffolk's brow the crown,
Debruising with a bloody bend
Poor Suffolk on her dexter end.
But Virtue from Olympian height
With due regard for What is Right
Decides it's Time to Interfere
And make the lawful issue clear.

Before the Bromley boy she sets
Deep pits disguised with shaky frets;
His easy path she makes a maze
And litters it with stags at gaze.
Poor Youth! Who finds that ev'ry place
is haunted by a leopard's face
Or watched by hordes of serpents nowed
Or dolphins naiant and embowed.

But flesh and blood can hardly bear
To face a griffin in its lair
When segreant from it's couch it rises
With gaping beak and awful noises:
Or when a chevron shouting fierce
Directs at one a pass in tierce
Or leopards, creeping on all fours
Show jessant lilies in their jaws.

Or when a bombard, burning bright
Sets one's best Sunday suit alight:
Or millrinds, grinding teeth in joy
Seek to devour th'intrepid boy.
Or when an ogress, munching hurt
And torteaux with her teeth of vert
Displays an over-burdened paunch
Crammed full of desiccated maunch.

Or saltires, sinister with vair
Encrined with wavy, undy hair:
Or nameless nombrils, honour dead
Unguled with toenails blue and red:
Or when a lion, double-queued,
Inspires a rather doubtful mood:
Or water bougets, stern and wild,
Drip ghastly drops of old and mild.

Cantons cavorting on a field
Will surely cause the lad to yield,
And who dare challenge—only fools—
An oak tree proper, fructed gules.
To mention naught of tressure flory—
That grim and somewhat painful story—
No more I'll say, except to add
That Circumstances beat the lad.

Virtue withdraws, her just task o'er.
The Boy his searches tries no more.
Sly Mistress Kent with hellish moan
Sinks back upon her Lesser throne.
And Mistress Suffolk calm, serene
Is still of all the Hatchments, Queen,
Secure amid her faithful swains
Hers is the glory their's the Brains.

[NB Final Score   Kent 344   Suffolk 302]

Appendix 5

Index Locorum

Please note that places with place names made up two words of a descriptive nature, e.g. Long, Great, High, East, West etc., are indexed here under the initial letter of the second word of the place

Abbey Dore, Vol.. 9, Herefordshire
Abbots Ripton, Vol. 6, Huntingdonshire
Abbotsbury, Vol. 7, Dorset
Abbotsleigh, Vol. 7, Somerset
Abbotts Ann, Vol. 7, Hampshire
Aberford, Vol. 3, Yorkshire
Abergavenny, Vol. 9, Monmouthshire
Aberystwyth, Nanteos House, Vol. 9, Wales
Abington Pigotts, Vol. 6, Cambridgeshire
Accrington, Vol. 3, Lancashire
Acton Scott, Vol. 9, Shropshire
Adbaston, Vol. 8, Staffordshire
Adel, Vol. 3, Yorkshire
Adlestrop, Vol. 7, Gloucestershire
Adlington Hall, Vol. 8, Cheshire
Adwick-Le-Street, Vol. 3, Yorkshire
Ainstable, Vol. 3, Cumberland
Alberbury, Vol. 9, Shropshire
Albury, St Peter & St Paul, Vol. 5, Surrey
Alby, Vol. 2, Norfolk
Aldborough, Vol. 3, Yorkshire
Aldbourne, Vol. 4, Wiltshire
Aldeburgh, Vol. 2, Suffolk
Alderley, Vol. 7, Gloucestershire
Aldermaston, Vol. 4, Berkshire
Alderwasley, Vol. 8, Derbyshire
Aldingbourne, Vol. 5, Sussex
Aldwincle, Vol. 1, Northamptonshire
Alfriston, Vol. 5, Sussex
Allerton Park, Vol. 3, Yorkshire
Almer, Vol. 7, Dorset
Alnwick, Vol. 3, Northumberland
Alresford, Vol. 6, Essex
Altham, Vol. 3, Lancashire
Alveston, Vol. 7, Gloucestershire
Alwington, Vol. 7, Devon
Amesbury, Vol. 4, Wiltshire
Ampton, Vol. 2, Suffolk
Amwell, Great, Vol. 6, Hertfordshire

Anmer, Vol. 2, Norfolk
Ansley, Vols. 1 & 10, Warwickshire
Anstey, Vol. 8, Leicestershire
Appleby Castle, Vol. 3, Westmorland
Appleton, Vol. 4, Berkshire
Ardington, Vol. 4, Berkshire
Arley, Vol. 1, Worcestershire
Armathwaithe, Vol. 3, Cumberland
Arrow, Vol. 1, Warwickshire
Arthuret, Vol. 3, Cumberland
Arundel, Castle, Vol. 5, Sussex
Arundel, The Fitzalan Chapel, Vol. 5, Sussex
Asgarby, Vol. 8, Lincolnshire
Ash, Vol. 5, Surrey
Ashburnham, Vol. 5, Sussex
Ashby Folville, Vol. 8, Leicestershire
Ashby St Ledgers, Vol. 1, Northampton-shire
Ashby-de-la-Launde, Vol. 8, Lincolnshire
Ashby-de-la-Zouch, Vols. 8 & 10, Leicestershire
Ashby-de-la-Zouch Museum, Vol. 10, Leicestershire
Ashfield, Great, Vol. 2, Suffolk
Ashford, Vol. 5, Kent
Ashley, Vols. 8 & 10, Staffordshire
Askham Bryan, Vol. 3, Yorkshire
Aspall, Vol. 2, Suffolk
Astley, Vol. 1, Worcestershire
Aston, Vol. 8, Cheshire
Aston Clinton, Vol. 4, Buckinghamshire
Aston Hall, Vol. 9, Shropshire
Aston-by-Stone, Vol. 8, Staffordshire
Aswarby, Vol. 8, Lincolnshire
Atcham, Vol. 9, Shropshire
Attenborough, Vol. 8, Nottinghamshire
Aubourn, Vol. 8, Lincolnshire
Auckland St Andrew, Vol. 3, Durham
Auckland St Helen, Vols. 3 & 10, Durham

Audley, Vol. 8, Staffordshire
Ault Hucknall, Vol. 8, Derbyshire
Aust, Vol. 7, Gloucestershire
Avebury, Vol. 4, Wiltshire
Averham, Vol. 8, Nottinghamshire
Avington, Vol. 4, Berkshire
Avington, Vol. 7, Hampshire
Aylesbury, County Museum, Vol. 4,
    Buckinghamshire
Aylesford, Vol. 5, Kent
Aylsham, Vols. 2 & 10, Norfolk

Babraham, Vol. 6, Cambridgeshire
Baddesley Clinton, Vols. 1 & 10,
    Warwickshire
Baddow, Great, Vol. 6, Essex
Badlesmere, Vol. 5, Kent
Badminton House, Vol. 7, Gloucestershire
Bagborough, Vol. 7, Somerset
Baildon, Vol. 3, Yorkshire
Bakewell Museum, Vol. 8, Derbyshire
Bamburgh, Vol. 3, Northumberland
Barcombe, Vol. 5, Sussex
Barden, Vol. 3 & 10, Yorkshire
Bardsey, Vols. 3 & 10, Yorkshire
Bardwell, Vol. 2, Suffolk
Barham, Vol. 2, Suffolk
Barkby, Vol. 8, Leicestershire
Barkham, Vol. 4, Berkshire
Barking, Vol. 2, Suffolk
Barkway, Vol. 6, Hertfordshire
Barlborough, Vol. 8, Derbyshire
Barnet, East, Vol. 6, Hertfordshire
Barningham Town, Vols. 2 & 10, Norfolk
Barrington, Vol. 6, Cambridgeshire
Barrow, Vol. 9, Shropshire
Barrow Gurney, Vol. 7, Somerset
Barrow-on-Trent, Vol. 8, Derbyshire
Barsham, Vol. 2, Suffolk
Barston, Vol. 1, Warwickshire
Barton Stacey, Vol. 7, Hampshire
Baschurch, Vol. 9, Shropshire
Basing, Old, Vol. 7, Hampshire
Basingstoke, Vol. 10, Hampshire
Bassaleg, Vol. 9, Monmouthshire
Bath, Masonic Temple, Vol. 7, Somerset
Bath, Private Possession, Vol. 10, Somerset
Battlefield, Vol. 9, Shropshire
Baumber, Vol. 8, Lincolnshire
Bayton, Vol. 1, Worcestershire
Beauchief Abbey, Sheffield, Vol. 3,
    Yorkshire
Bebington, St Andrew, Vol. 8, Cheshire
Beccles, Vol. 2, Suffolk
Bedford Museum, Vol. 4, Bedfordshire
Bedingfield, Vol. 2, Suffolk
Bedingham, Vol. 2, Norfolk
Bedwyn, Great, Vols. 4 & 10, Wiltshire
Beeston, Vol. 8, Nottinghamshire
Beeston St Lawrence, Vol. 2, Norfolk

Beeston-Next-Mileham, Vols. 2 & 10,
    Norfolk
Belsay Castle, Vol. 3, Northumberland
Benacre, Vol. 2, Suffolk
Benefield, Vol. 1, Northamptonshire
Bengeo, Vol. 6, Hertfordshire
Benhall, Vol. 2, Suffolk
Benthall, Vol. 9, Shropshire
Beoley, Vol. 1, Worcestershire
Berechurch, Vol. 6, Essex
Berkhamsted, Vol. 6, Hertfordshire
Berkswell, Vol. 1, Warwickshire
Bermondsey, Vol. 5, Surrey
Berrington, Vol. 9, Shropshire
Berwick, Vol. 9, Shropshire
Berwick St John, Vols. 4 & 10, Wiltshire
Besford, Vol. 1, Worcestershire
Bessels Leigh, Vol. 4, Berkshire
Betchworth, Vol. 5, Surrey
Betley, Vol. 8, Staffordshire
Betton Strange, Vol. 9, Shropshire
Bettws, Vol. 9, Wales
Beverley Minster, Vol. 10, Yorkshire
Bewdley, Vol. 1, Worcestershire
Bexley, Vol. 5, Kent
Bicton, Vol. 7, Devon
Bicton, Vol. 9, Shropshire
Biddlesden, Vol. 4, Buckinghamshire
Biddulph, Vol. 8, Staffordshire
Bideford, Vol. 7, Devon
Bigland Hall nr Cartmel, Vol. 3, Lanca-
    shire
Billinge, Vol. 3, Lancashire
Bilsington, Vol. 5, Kent
Bilton, Vol. 1, Warwickshire
Binbrook, Vol. 8, Lincolnshire
Binghams Melcombe, Vol. 7, Dorset
Bingley, Vol. 3, Yorkshire
Birdbrook, Vol. 6, Essex
Birling, Vol. 5, Kent
Birmingham, St Chads, Vol. 1, Warwick-
    shire
Birtsmorton, Vol. 1, Worcestershire
Bishop Burton, Vol. 3, Yorkshire
Bishopthorpe, Vol. 3, Yorkshire
Bishop's Lydeard, Vol. 7, Somerset
Bishop's Stortford, Vol. 6, Hertfordshire
Bishop's Waltham, Vol. 7, Hampshire
Bisterne, Vol. 7, Hampshire
Bitton, Vol. 7, Gloucestershire
Black Notley, Vol. 6, Essex
Blackawton, Vol. 7, Devon
Blackheath, Morden Coll Chapel, Vol. 5,
    Kent
Blandford, Vol. 7, Dorset
Blatherwick, Vol. 1, Northamptonshire
Bletsoe, Vol. 4, Bedfordshire
Blewbury, Vol. 4, Berkshire
Blickling Hall, Vol. 2, Norfolk
Blunham, Vol. 4, Bedfordshire

Cadeby, Vol. 8, Leicestershire
Caister, Vol. 2, Norfolk
Calbourne, Vol. 7, Isle of Wight
Calke, Vol. 8, Derbyshire
Cambridge, King's College, Vol. 6,
    Cambridgeshire
Cambridge, Magdalene College, Vol. 6,
    Cambridgeshire
Cambridge, St John's College, Vol. 6,
    Cambridgeshire
Campton, Vol. 4, Bedfordshire
Canewdon, Vol. 6, Essex
Canon Frome, Vol. 9, Herefordshire
Canons Ashby, Vol. 1, Northamptonshire
Canterbury, Holy Cross, Vol. 5, Kent
Canterbury, St Mildred, Vol. 5, Kent
Canterbury, St Stephen, Hack, Vol. 5, Kent
Canwick, Vol. 8, Lincolnshire
Capel Llanilterne, Vol. 9, Wales
Capesthorne Hall, Vol. 8, Cheshire
Car Colston, Vol. 8, Nottinghamshire
Cardiff, Welsh Folk Museum, Vol. 9,
    Wales
Carisbrooke, Vol. 7, Isle of Wight
Carlton, East, Vol. 1, Northamptonshire
Carlton, South, Vol. 8, Lincolnshire
Carlton Towers, nr Selby, Vol. 3, Yorkshire
Carlton-in-Lindrick, Vol. 8, Nottingham-
    shire
Carlton-next-Kelsale, Vol. 2, Suffolk
Cartmel, Vol. 3, Lancashire
Castle Combe, Vol. 4, Wiltshire
Castleton, Vol. 8, Derbyshire
Catesby, Vol. 1, Northamptonshire
Catterick, Vol. 3, Yorkshire
Catton, Vol. 2, Norfolk
Catworth, Vol. 6, Huntingdonshire
Cave, North, Vol. 3, Yorkshire
Cerney, North, Vol. 7, Gloucestershire
Chale, Blackgang Chine Museum, Vol. 7,
    Isle of Wight
Chalfont St Giles, Vol. 4, Buckingham-
    shire
Chalfont St Peter, Vol. 4, Buckinghamshire
Chalvington, Vol. 5, Sussex
Chapel-en-le-Frith, Vol. 8, Derbyshire
Chardstock, Vol. 7, Devon
Charlecote, Vol. 1, Warwickshire
Charlton Musgrove, Vol. 7, Somerset
Charlton, Nr Woolwich, Vol. 5, Kent
Charsfield, Vol. 2, Suffolk
Chart, Great, Vol. 5, Kent
Chastleton House, Vol. 4, Oxfordshire
Chatteris, Vol. 6, Cambridgeshire
Chedzoy, Vol. 7, Somerset
Chelsea, Old Church, Vol. 10, Middlesex
Chelsham, Vol. 5, Surrey
Chelsworth, Vol. 2, Suffolk
Chenies, Vol. 4, Buckinghamshire
Chequers, Vol. 4, Buckinghamshire

Cheriton, Vol. 7, Hampshire
Cherry Burton, Vol. 3, Yorkshire
Chesham, Vol. 4, Buckinghamshire
Chesham Bois, Vol. 4, Buckinghamshire
Chesterton, Vol. 6, Huntingdonshire
Chester, St John, Vol. 8, Cheshire
Chetwode, Vol. 4, Buckinghamshire
Chevening, Vol. 5, Kent
Chickney, Vol. 6, Essex
Chiddingfold, Vol. 5, Surrey
Chiddingly, Vol. 5, Sussex
Chiddingstone, Vol. 5, Kent
Chigwell, Vol. 6, Essex
Childwall, Vols. 3 & 10, Lancashire
Chilham, Vol. 5, Kent
Chilton Foliat, Vol. 4, Wiltshire
Chingford, All Saints, Vol. 6, Essex
Chingford, SS Peter and Paul, Vols. 6 &
    10, Essex
Chippenham, Vol. 6, Cambridgeshire
Chipping Barnet, Vol. 6, Hertfordshire
Chirbury, Vol. 9, Shropshire
Chirk, Vol. 9, Wales
Chirton, Vol. 4, Wiltshire
Chiselhampton, Vol. 4, Oxfordshire
Chislehurst, Vol. 5, Kent
Chislet, Vol. 5, Kent
Chobham, Vol. 5, Surrey
Cholmondeley Castle, Vols. 8 & 10,
    Cheshire
Christchuch-on-Needwood, Vol. 8,
    Staffordshire
Christchurch, Vol. 7, Hampshire
Church Gresley, Vol. 8, Derbyshire
Church Minshull, Vol. 8, Cheshire
City of London, St Dunstan's, Vol. 6,
    Middlesex
City of London, St James, Gar, Vol. 6,
    Middlesex
Clandon East, Vol. 5, Surrey
Clandon Park, Vol. 5, Surrey
Clare, Vol. 2, Suffolk
Claverley, Vol. 9, Shropshire
Claverton, Vol. 7, Somerset
Cleobury, North, Vol. 9, Shropshire
Clewer, Vo. 10, Berkshire
Clifton Reynes, Vol. 4, Buckinghamshire
Clitheroe, Vol. 3, Lancashire
Clowne, Vol. 8, Derbyshire
Clungunford, Vol. 9, Shropshire
Clyro, Vol. 9, Wales
Coker, East, Coker Court, Vol. 7, Somerset
Coddenham, Vol. 2, Suffolk
Codford St Peter, Vol. 4, Wiltshire
Coggeshall, Vol. 6, Essex
Colchester, Castle Museum, Vol. 6, Essex
Colchester, Holy Trinity, Vol. 6, Essex
Colchester, St James, Vol. 6, Essex
Collingham, Vol. 3, Yorkshire
Colne, Vol. 3, Lancashire

Ecton Hall, Vol. 1, Northamptonshire
Edgmond, Vol. 9, Shropshire
Edgton, Vol. 9, Shropshire
Edgware, Vol. 6, Middlesex
Edith Weston, Vol. 8, Rutland
Edmondthorpe, Vol. 8, Leicestershire
Edmonton, All Saints, Vol. 6, Middlesex
Edmonton, St James, Fore St, Vol. 6,
  Middlesex
Eggington, Vol. 8, Derbyshire
Egglescliffe, Vol. 3, Durham
Egham, Vol. 5, Surrey
Egton, Vol. 3, Yorkshire
Eling, Vol. 7, Hampshire
Ellingham, Vol. 7, Hampshire
Ellingham, Vols. 2 & 10, Norfolk
Elmdon, Vol. 1, Warwickshire
Elmham, North, Vols. 2 & 10,
  Norfolk
Elmley Lovett, Vol. 1, Worcestershire
Elmore, Vol. 7, Gloucestershire
Elmsett, Vol. 2, Suffolk
Elsenham, Vol. 6, Essex
Elsing Hall, Vol. 2, Norfolk
Elstow, Vol. 4, Bedfordshire
Elton, Vol. 8, Nottinghamshire
Elvaston, Vol. 8, Derbyshire
Elvetham, Vol. 7, Hampshire
Embleton, Vol. 3, Northumberland
Empingham, Vol. 8, Rutland
Enderby, Vol. 8, Leicestershire
Enford, Vol. 4, Wiltshire
Enham Alamein, Vol. 7, Hampshire
Enville, Vol. 8, Staffordshire
Erddig, Vol. 9, Wales
Esher, St George, Vol. 5, Surrey
Eton College, Vol. 4, Buckinghamshire
Ettington, Vol. 1, Warwickshire
Etwall, Vol. 8, Derbyshire
Evercreech, Vols. 7 & 10, Somerset
Everdon, Vol. 1, Northamptonshire
Everleigh, Vol. 4, Wiltshire
Everton, Vol. 6, Huntingdonshire
Exminster, Vol. 7, Devon
Eye, Vol. 9, Herefordshire
Eye, Vol. 2, Suffolk

Faringdon, Vol. 4, Berkshire
Farleigh Hungerford, Vol. 7, Somerset
Farley, Vol. 4, Wiltshire
Farley Chamberlayne, Vol. 7, Hampshire
Farnham, Vol. 5, Surrey
Farnworth nr Widnes, Vols. 3 & 10,
  Lancashire
Fawsley, Vol. 1, Northamptonshire
Felbrigg, Vol. 2, Norfolk
Feniscowles, Vol. 10, Lancashire
Fillongley, Vol. 1, Warwickshire
Finchingfield, Vol. 6, Essex
Finchley, Vol. 6, Middlesex

Finchley, East, Holy Trinity, Vol. 6,
  Middlesex
Firbeck, Vol. 3, Yorkshire
Fladbury, Vol. 1, Worcestershire
Flamstead, Vol. 6, Hertfordshire
Fletching, Vol. 5, Sussex
Flintham, Vol. 8, Nottinghamshire
Folke, Vol. 7, Dorset
Fordcombe, Vol. 5, Kent
Forde Abbey, Vol. 7, Dorset
Fordham, Vol. 6, Cambridgeshire
Fordwich, Vol. 5, Kent
Foremark, Vol. 8, Derbyshire
Fornham All Saints, Vol. 2, Suffolk
Fornham St Martin, Vol. 2, Suffolk
Forton, Vol. 8, Staffordshire
Fowey, Vol. 7, Cornwall
Framlingham, Vol. 2, Suffolk
Frampton-on-Severn, Vol. 7,
  Gloucestershire
Freefolk, Vol. 7, Hampshire
Fremington, Vol. 7, Devon
Fretherne, Vol. 7, Gloucestershire
Friern Barnet, Vol. 6, Middlesex
Friskney, Vol. 8, Lincolnshire
Frodesley, Vol. 9, Shropshire
Froyle, Vol. 7, Hampshire
Fulbourn, Vol. 6, Cambridgeshire
Fulford, St Oswald, York, Vol. 3, Yorkshire
Fulmer, Vol. 4, Buckinghamshire
Fylingdales, Old Church, Vol. 3, Yorkshire

Gaddesden, Great, Vol. 10, Hertfordshire
Gainford, Vol. 3, Durham
Gainsborough, Old Hall, Vol. 8, Lincoln-
  shire
Garboldisham, Vol. 2, Norfolk
Garton, Vol. 3, Yorkshire
Gatton, Vol. 5, Surrey
Gayhurst, Vol. 4, Buckinghamshire
Gedling, Vol. 8, Nottinghamshire
Gestingthorpe, Vol. 6, Essex
Gibside Chapel, Vol. 3, Durham
Giggleswick, Vol. 3, Yorkshire
Gillingham, Vol. 7, Dorset
Gipping, Vol. 2, Suffolk
Gisburn, Vol. 3, Yorkshire
Gittisham, Vol. 7, Devon
Glasson, Vol. 3, Lancashire
Glynde, Vol. 5, Sussex
Goathurst, Vol. 7, Somerset
Godshill, Vol. 7, Isle of Wight
Goosnargh, Vol. 3, Lancashire
Goring, Vol. 5, Sussex
Gosfield, Vol. 6, Essex
Grafton Flyford, Vol. 1, Worcestershire
Grainsby, Vol. 8, Lincolnshire
Grantham, Vol. 8, Lincolnshire
Grasmere, Vol. 3, Westmorland
Grendon, Vol. 1, Northamptonshire

Hockering, Vols. 2 & 10, Norfolk
Holbrook, Vol. 2, Suffolk
Hollingbourne, Vol. 5, Kent
Holme Lacy, Vol. 9, Herefordshire
Holt, Vol. 4, Wiltshire
Holywell, Vol. 6, Huntingdonshire
Honing, Vol. 2, Norfolk
Honingham, Vol. 2, Norfolk
Honington, Vol. 1, Warwickshire
Hoole, Vols. 3 & 10, Lancashire
Hooton Pagnall, Vol. 3, Yorkshire
Hope, Vol. 10, Derbyshire
Hopton Wafers, Vol. 9, Shropshire
Horbling, Vol. 8, Lincolnshire
Horbury, Vol. 3, Yorkshire
Horham Hall, nr Thaxted, Vols. 6 & 10,
    Essex
Horkesley, Great, Vol. 6, Essex
Horkstow, Vol. 8, Lincolnshire
Horley, Vol. 4, Oxfordshire
Hornby, Vol. 3, Lancashire
Horncastle, Vol. 8, Lincolnshire
Horsham, Vol. 5, Sussex
Horsington, Vol. 7, Somerset
Horsley, East, Vol. 5, Surrey
Horton, Vol. 7, Gloucestershire
Horton, Vol. 1, Northamptonshire
Horton Kirby, Vol. 5, Kent
Horwich, Vol. 3, Lancashire
Houghton, Vols. 2 & 10, Norfolk
Houghton Regis, Vol. 4, Bedfordshire
Hoveton St John, Vols. 2 & 10, Norfolk
Hoveton St Peter, Vols. 2 & 10, Norfolk
Howden, Vol. 3, Yorkshire
Hucknall Torkard, Vol. 8, Nottinghamshire
Hulland, Vol. 8, Derbyshire
Humberston, Vol. 8, Lincolnshire
Hungarton, Vol. 8, Leicestershire
Hunmanby, Vols. 3 & 10, Yorkshire
Hunston, Vol. 2, Suffolk
Huntingfield, Vol. 2, Suffolk
Husbands Bosworth, Old Hall, Vol. 8,
    Leicestershire
Husborne Crawley, Vol. 4, Bedfordshire
Hutton-in-the-Forest, Vol. 3, Cumberland

Ickleford, Vol. 6, Hertfordshire
Ightham, Vol. 5, Kent
Ightham Mote, Vol. 5, Kent
Ilford, Little, Vol. 6, Essex
Ince, Vol. 8, Cheshire
Ingleby Greenhow, Vol. 3, Yorkshire
Iping, Vol. 5, Sussex
Ipplepen, Vol. 7, Devon
Ipswich, Christchurch Museum, Vol. 2,
    Suffolk
Ipswich, St Margaret's, Vol. 2, Suffolk
Ipswich, St Mary Elm's, Vol. 2, Suffolk
Ipswich, St Peter, Vol. 2, Suffolk
Ipswich, St Stephen, Vol. 2, Suffolk

Irnham, Vol. 8, Lincolnshire
Isleham, Vol. 6, Cambridgeshire
Itton, Vol. 9, Monmouthshire
Iwerne Minster, Vol. 7, Dorset

Kedington, Vol. 2, Suffolk
Kedleston, Vol. 8, Derbyshire
Kellet Over, Vol. 3, Lancashire
Kelsale, Vol. 2, Suffolk
Kelston, Vol. 7, Somerset
Kempston, Vol. 4, Bedfordshire
Kennington, Vol. 5, Kent
Kenton, Vol. 7, Devon
Kersey, Vol. 2, Suffolk
Kesgrave, Vol. 2 & 10, Suffolk
Ketteringham, Vol. 2, Norfolk
Kew, Vols. 5 & 10, Surrey
Keynsham, Vol. 7, Somerset
Kidderminster, Vol. 1, Worcestershire
Kidlington, Vol. 4, Oxfordshire
Kilham, Vol. 3, Yorkshire
Kilmington, Vol. 4, Wiltshire
Kilnwick, Vol. 3, Yorkshire
Kimbolton, Vol. 6, Huntingdonshire
Kingham, Vol. 4, Oxfordshire
Kings Norton, Vol. 1, Warwickshire
Kingsbury, Vol. 1, Warwickshire
Kingston, Vol. 5, Kent
Kingston Lisle, Vol. 4, Berkshire
Kingston St Mary, Vol. 7, Somerset
Kingston Vale, Vol. 5, Surrey
Kingston-upon-Thames, Vol. 5, Surrey
Kingsworthy, Vol. 7, Hampshire
King's Walden, Vol. 6, Hertfordshire
Kinsham, Vol. 9, Herefordshire
Kirby Cane, Vol. 2, Norfolk
Kirdford, Vol. 5, Sussex
Kirk Hallam, Vol. 8, Derbyshire
Kirkby Mallory, Vol. 8, Leicestershire
Kirkheaton, Vol. 3, Yorkshire
Kirkleatham, Vols. 3 & 10, Yorkshire
Kirkleatham Old Hall Museum, Vols. 3 &
    10, Yorkshire
Kirklington, Vol. 3, Yorkshire
Kirstead, Vol. 2, Norfolk
Kirtling, Vol. 6, Cambridgeshire
Kirtlington, Vol. 4, Oxfordshire
Knaresborough, Vol. 3, Yorkshire
Knebworth, Vol. 6, Hertfordshire
Knighton, Vol. 8, Leicestershire
Knill, Vol. 9, Herefordshire
Knole House, Vol. 5, Kent
Knowlton, Vol. 5, Kent
Knutsford, Vol. 8, Cheshire
Kyre Wyard, Vol. 1, Worcestershire

Lacey Green, Vol. 4, Buckinghamshire
Lacock Abbey, Vol. 4, Wiltshire
Laleham, Vol. 6, Middlesex
Lamberhurst, Vol. 5, Kent

Lymington, Vol. 7, Hampshire
Lymm, Vol. 8, Cheshire
Lympsham, Vol. 7, Somerset
Lynsted, Vol. 5, Kent
Lytchett Matravers, Vol. 7, Dorset

Macclesfield, Vol. 8, Cheshire
Machynlleth, Vol. 9, Wales
Madron, Vol. 7, Cornwall
Maidstone, All Saints, Vol. 5, Kent
Maidstone, Museum, Vol. 5, Kent
Maldon, Vol. 6, Essex
Malmesbury, Vol. 4, Wiltshire
Malpas, Vol. 8, Cheshire
Malvern Priory, Little, Vols. 1 & 10,
    Worcestershire
Mancetter, Vol. 1, Warwickshire
Mapledurham, Vol. 4, Oxfordshire
Mappleton, Vols. 3 & 10, Yorkshire
Mareham-on-the-Hill, Vol. 8, Lincolnshire
Margam Abbey, Vol. 9, Wales
Margaretting, Vol. 6, Essex
Margate, Vols. 5 & 10, Kent
Market Bosworth, Vol. 8, Leicestershire
Market Lavington, Vol. 4, Wiltshire
Marlesford, Vol. 2, Suffolk
Marlingford, Vols. 2 & 10, Norfolk
Marlow, Vol. 4, Buckinghamshire
Marnhull, Vol. 7, Dorset
Marrick Priory, Vols. 3 & 10, Yorkshire
Marsh Baldon, Vol. 4, Oxfordshire
Marske-by-the-Sea, Vol. 3, Yorkshire
Marston, Vol. 8, Lincolnshire
Marston Morteyne, Vol. 4, Bedfordshire
Marston Trussel, Vol. 1, Northamptonshire
Martin, Vol. 7, Hampshire
Martlesham, Vol. 2, Suffolk
Marton, East, Vol. 3, Yorkshire
Marylebone, St Mary, Vol. 6, Middlesex
Masham, Vol. 3, Yorkshire
Massingham, Great, Vol. 2, Norfolk
Matlask, Vol. 2, Norfolk
Matlock, St Giles, Vol. 8, Derbyshire
Mavesyn Ridware, Vol. 8, Staffordshire
Maxstoke, Vols. 1 & 10, Warwickshire
Medmenham, Vol. 4, Buckinghamshire
Melbourne, Vols. 8 & 10, Derbyshire
Melbury House, Vol. 7, Dorset
Melford Hall, Vol. 10, Suffolk
Melford, Long, Vol. 2, Suffolk
Melksham, Vol. 4, Wiltshire
Melling, Vol. 3, Lancashire
Melmerby, Vol. 3, Cumberland
Melton Mowbray, Vol. 8, Leicestershire
Melton (Old Church), Vol. 2, Suffolk
Mendlesham, Vol. 2, Suffolk
Mentmore, Vol. 4, Buckinghamshire
Meopham, Vol. 5, Kent
Mere, Vol. 4, Wiltshire
Merevale, Vol. 1, Warwickshire

Mersham, Vol. 5, Kent
Merton, Vol. 5, Surrey
Messing, Vol. 6, Essex
Methley, Vol. 3, Yorkshire
Micheldever, Vol. 7, Hampshire
Mickleham, Vol. 5, Surrey
Mickleton, Vol. 7, Gloucestershire
Middleton Cheyney, Vol. 1, Northampton-
    shire
Middleton Tyas, Vol. 3, Yorkshire
Midsomer Norton, R C Church, Vol. 7,
    Somerset
Milborne Port, Vol. 7, Somerset
Mildenhall, Vol. 4, Wiltshire
Millom, Vol. 3, Cumberland
Milton Bryan, Vol. 4, Bedfordshire
Milton Manor, Vol. 4, Berkshire
Milton, nr Gravesend, Vol. 5, Kent
Milverton, Vol. 1, Warwickshire
Minster-in-Sheppey, Vol. 5, Kent
Miserden, Vol. 7, Gloucestershire
Mitton, Great, Vols. 3 & 10, Yorkshire
Modbury, Vol. 7, Devon
Monks Kirby, Vol. 1, Warwickshire
Monkton, Vol. 5, Kent
Montgomery, Vol. 9, Wales
Moor Monkton, Red House, Vol. 3,
    Yorkshire
Morcott, Vol. 8, Rutland
Morden, Vol. 7, Dorset
Morden, Vol. 5, Surrey
More, Vol. 9, Shropshire
Morland, Vol. 3, Westmorland
Mortlake, Vol. 5, Surrey
Morton, Vol. 8, Derbyshire
Morville, Vol. 9, Shropshire
Motcombe, Vol. 7, Dorset
Mottram, Hall Farm, Vol. 8, Cheshire
Moulton, Vol. 8, Lincolnshire
Much Marcle, Vol. 9, Herefordshire
Mulbarton, Vol. 2, Norfolk
Munden Little, Vol. 6, Hertfordshire
Mundford, Vol. 2, Norfolk
Muskham, North, Vol. 8, Nottinghamshire
Myddfai, Vol. 9, Wales
Myddle, Vol. 9, Shropshire
Mylor, Vol. 7, Cornwall
Myton-Upon-Swale, Vol. 3, Yorkshire

Nailsea Court, Vol. 7, Somerset
Narborough, Vol. 2, Norfolk
Narford, Vol. 2, Norfolk
Nash, Vol. 9, Shropshire
Nazeing, Vol. 6, Essex
Neath, Vol. 9, Wales
Ness, Great, Vol. 9, Shropshire
Nether Winchendon, Vol. 4, Buckingham-
    shire
Nevill Holt, Vol. 8, Leicestershire
Newton Long, Vol. 3, Durham

Powerstock, Vol. 7, Dorset
Preshute, Vol. 4, Wiltshire
Preston Deanery, Vol. 1, Northamptonshire
Preston-on-Stour, Vol. 1, Warwickshire
Prestwold, Vol. 8, Leicestershire
Private Possession, Vol. 1, Worcestershire
Private Possession, Vol. 1, Worcestershire
Private Possession, Vol. 2, Norfolk
Private Possession, Vol. 10, Hertfordshire
Private Possession, Vol. 10, Lancashire
Private Possession, Vol. 10, Somerset
Probus, Trewithen House, Vols. 7 & 10,
  Cornwall
Purleigh, Vol. 6, Essex
Purse Caundle, Vol. 7, Dorset
Pusey, Vol. 4, Berkshire
Puttenham, Vol. 6, Hertfordshire

Quatt, Vol. 9, Shropshire
Queen Camel, Vol. 7, Somerset
Queenhill, Vol. 1, Worcestershire
Quenby Hall, Vol. 8, Leicestershire
Quy, Vols. 6 & 10, Cambridgeshire

Radbourne, Vol. 8, Derbyshire
Radley, Vol. 4, Berkshire
Radnor, Old, Vol. 9, Wales
Raynham, East, Vol. 2, Norfolk
Rampton, Vol. 8, Nottinghamshire
Ramsden Bellhouse, Vol. 6, Essex
Ramsey, Vol. 6, Essex
Ramsgate, St Lawrence, Vol. 5, Kent
Ravenfield, Vol. 3, Yorkshire
Ravensthorp, Vol. 1, Northamptonshire
Redbourne, Vol. 6, Hertfordshire
Redgrave, Vol. 2, Suffolk
Renishaw Hall, Vol. 8, Derbyshire
Reynham, Vols. 6 & 10, Essex
Riby, Vol. 8, Lincolnshire
Richards Castle, Vol. 9, Herefordshire
Richmond Museum, Vols. 3 & 10,
  Yorkshire
Ridge, Vol. 6, Hertfordshire
Ringland, Vol. 2, Norfolk
Ringmer, Vol. 5, Sussex
Ringwood, Vol. 7, Hampshire
Ripley, Vol. 3, Yorkshire
Ripon Cathedral, Vol. 3, Yorkshire
Ripple, Vol. 5, Kent
Rivenhall, Vol. 6, Essex
Riverhead, Vol. 5, Kent
Rock Hall, Vol. 3, Northumberland
Rockland St Mary, Vol. 2, Norfolk
Rockland St Mary, Vol. 10, Norfolk
Rodden, Vol. 7, Somerset
Rolvenden, Vol. 5, Kent
Romsey, Vol. 7, Hampshire
Ropley, Vol. 7, Hampshire
Ross-on-Wye, Harewood House Chapel,
  Vol. 9, Herefordshire

Rothbury, Vol. 3, Northumberland
Rothley, Temple Chapel, Vol. 8,
  Leicestershire
Rothwell, Vol. 1, Northamptonshire
Rousham, Vols. 4 & 10, Oxfordshire
Rowley, Vol. 10, Yorkshire
Roydon, Vol. 6, Essex
Ruabon, Vol. 9, Wales
Rugeley, Vols. 8 & 10, Staffordshire
Ruislip, Vol. 6, Middlesex
Runcton, North, Vol. 2, Norfolk
Rushall, Vol. 4, Wiltshire
Rushbrooke, Vol. 2, Suffolk
Rushton Manor, Vol. 1, Northamptonshire
Rushton Spencer, Vol. 8, Staffordshire
Ruyton-of-the-XI-Towns, Vol. 9, Shrop-
  shire
Ryde, St Thomas, Vols. 7 & 10, Isle of
  Wight
Ryder Hall, Vol. 10, Dorset
Rye, Vol. 5, Sussex
Ryston, Vol. 2, Norfolk
Ryton, Vol. 3, Durham

Salehurst, Vol. 5, Sussex
Salhouse, Vol. 2, Norfolk
Salisbury, St Edmund, Vol. 4, Wiltshire
Salisbury, St Martin, Vol. 4, Wiltshire
Salisbury, St Thomas, Vol. 4, Wiltshire
Sall, Vol. 2, Norfolk
Saltmarshe Castle, Vol. 9, Herefordshire
Sampford, Little, Vol. 6, Essex
Sampford Spiney, Vol. 7, Devon
Sandal Magna, Vols. 3 & 10, Yorkshire
Sandbeck Hall Chapel, Vol. 3, Yorkshire
Sandford St Martin, Vol. 4, Oxfordshire
Sandon, Vol. 6, Essex
Sandon, Vol. 8, Staffordshire
Sandringham, Vol. 2, Norfolk
Sandwich, Guildhall, Vol. 5, Kent
Sandwich, St Clement, Vol. 5, Kent
Sandwich, St Mary, Vol. 5, Kent
Sandwich, St Peter, Vol. 5, Kent
Santon Downham, Vol. 2, Suffolk
Sarnesfield, Vol. 9, Herefordshire
Sawbridgeworth, Vol. 6, Hertfordshire
Sawston Hall, Vol. 6, Cambridgeshire
Saxby, Vol. 8, Lincolnshire
Scawby, Vol. 8, Lincolnshire
Scotton, Vol. 8, Lincolnshire
Scottow, Vol. 2, Norfolk
Scoulton, Vol. 2, Norfolk
Scraptoft, Vol. 8, Leicestershire
Seale, Vol. 5, Surrey
Seaton Delaval, Vol. 3, Northumberland
Sedlescombe, Vol. 5, Sussex
Seend, Vol. 4, Wiltshire
Sefton, Vol. 3, Lancashire
Seighford, Vol. 8, Staffordshire

Stockport, Vol. 8, Cheshire
Stoke Bruern, Vol. 1, Northamptonshire
Stoke Edith, Vol. 9, Herefordshire
Stoke Gifford, Vol. 7, Gloucestershire
Stoke North, Vol. 4, Oxfordshire
Stoke Poges, Vol. 4, Buckinghamshire
Stoke Richard, Vol. 8, Lincolnshire
Stonehouse, Vol. 7, Gloucestershire
Stoneleigh, Vol. 1, Warwickshire
Stonham Aspall, Vol. 2, Suffolk
Stonor Park, Vol. 4, Oxfordshire
Stopham, Vol. 5, Sussex
Stoulton, Vol. 1, Worcestershire
Stourbridge, Oldswinford Hosp, Vol. 1,
    Worcestershire
Stow Bardolph, Vol. 2, Norfolk
Stowe, Vol. 4, Buckinghamshire
Stowlangtoft, Vol. 2, Suffolk
Stowmarket, Vol. 2, Suffolk
Stratfield Saye, Vol. 7, Hampshire
Stratford-on-Avon, Vols. 1 & 10,
    Warwickshire
Stratton, East, Vol. 7, Hampshire
Stratton, Long, Vol. 2, Norfolk
Strensham, Vol. 1, Worcestershire
Strethall, Vol. 6, Essex
Stukeley, Great, Vol. 6, Huntingdonshire
Studland, Vol. 7, Dorset
Studley, Vol. 1, Warwickshire
Stutton, Vol. 2, Suffolk
Sudbourne, Vol. 2, Suffolk
Sunderland Museum, Vol. 10,
    Durham
Sundridge, Vol. 5, Kent
Surfleet, Vol. 8, Lincolnshire
Sutton, Vol. 6, Essex
Sutton-at-Hone, Vol. 5, Kent
Sutton-in-Ashfield, Vol. 8, Nottinghamshire
Swaffham Prior, Vol. 6, Cambridgeshire
Swalcliffe, Vol. 4, Oxfordshire
Swannington, Vols. 2 & 10, Norfolk
Swerford, Vol. 4, Oxfordshire
Swettenham, Vols. 8 & 10, Cheshire
Swindon, Holy Rood, Vol. 4, Wiltshire
Swinford, Vols. 8 & 10, Leicestershire
Swinhope, Vol. 8, Lincolnshire
Swithland, Vol. 8, Leicestershire
Sydling St Nicholas, Vol. 7, Dorset
Tacolneston, Vol. 2, Norfolk
Tadcaster, Vol. 3, Yorkshire
Talgarth, Vol. 9, Wales
Tamerton Foliot, Vol. 7, Devon
Tamworth Castle, Vol. 8, Staffordshire
Tannington, Vol. 2, Suffolk
Tatsfield, Vol. 5, Surrey
Tatton Park, Vol. 8, Cheshire
Taunton Museum, Vol. 7, Somerset
Tawstock, Vol. 7, Devon
Tealby, Vol. 8, Lincolnshire

Teignmouth, St James, Vol. 7, Devon
Temple Balsall, Vol. 1, Warwickshire
Temple Guiting, Vol. 7, Gloucestershire
Temple Newsam House, Vols. 3 & 10,
    Yorkshire
Tempsford, Vol. 4, Bedfordshire
Terling, Vol. 6, Essex
Terrington St Clements, Vol. 2, Norfolk
Teston, Vol. 5, Kent
Teversal, Vol. 8, Nottinghamshire
Tew, Great, Vol. 4, Oxfordshire
Thaxted, Vols. 6 & 10, Essex
Theberton, Vol. 2, Suffolk
Thenford, Vol. 1, Northamptonshire
Theydon Bois, Vol. 6, Essex
Theydon Garnon, Vol. 6, Essex
Theydon Mount, Vol. 6, Essex
Thirsk, Vol. 3, Yorkshire
Thorganby, Vol. 8, Lincolnshire
Thorington, Vol. 2, Suffolk
Thornbury, Vol. 7, Gloucestershire
Thorncombe, Vol. 7, Dorset
Thorney, Vol. 8, Nottinghamshire
Thornfalcon, Vol. 7, Somerset
Thornham Magna, Vol. 2, Suffolk
Thornton Watlass, Vol. 3, Yorkshire
Thornton-le-Moors, Vol. 8, Cheshire
Thornton-Le-Street, Vol. 3, Yorkshire
Thorp Malsor Hall, Vol. 1, Northampton-
    shire
Thorpe Morieux, Vol. 2, Suffolk
Thorpe St Andrew, Vols. 2 & 10, Norfolk
Thorpe Thewles, Vol. 3, Durham
Thrandeston, Vol. 2, Suffolk
Throwley, Vol. 5, Kent
Thundridge, Vols. 6 & 10, Hertfordshire
Thurleigh, Vol. 4, Bedfordshire
Thurlow, Little, Vol. 2, Suffolk
Tibenham, Vol. 2, Norfolk
Tichborne, Vol. 7, Hampshire
Tickencote, Vol. 8, Rutland
Tideswell, Vol. 8, Derbyshire
Tillington, Vol. 5, Sussex
Tilty, Vol. 6, Essex
Tingrith, Vol. 4, Bedfordshire
Tissington, Vol. 8, Derbyshire
Titsey, Vol. 5, Surrey
Tittleshall, Vol. 2, Norfolk
Tixover, Vol. 8, Rutland
Tockenham, Vol. 4, Wiltshire
Toddington, Vol. 4, Bedfordshire
Todenham, Vol. 7, Gloucestershire
Toftrees, Vol. 2, Norfolk
Tollerton, Vol. 8, Nottinghamshire
Tonbridge, Vol. 5, Kent
Tong, Vols. 3 & 10, Yorkshire
Topcroft, Vol. 2, Norfolk
Topsham, Vol. 7, Devon
Tortington, Vol. 5, Sussex

Wickwar, Vol. 7, Gloucestershire
Wigan, Vol. 3, Lancashire
Wighill, Vol. 3, Yorkshire
Wigmore, Vol. 9, Herefordshire
Wilby, Vol. 2, Suffolk
Willesden, Vol. 6, Middlesex
Willesley, Vols. 8 & 10, Leicestershire
Willey, Vol. 9, Shropshire
Willington, Vol. 8, Derbyshire
Wilmington, Vol. 5, Kent
Wilsford, nr Amesbury, Vol. 4, Wiltshire
Wilsthorpe, Vol. 8, Lincolnshire
Wilton, Vol. 4, Wiltshire
Winch, East, Vol. 2, Norfolk
Winchelsea, Vol. 5, Sussex
Winchester Cathedral, Vol. 7, Hampshire
Winchester College, Vol. 7, Hampshire
Winchester, Hampshire Record Office, Vol.
    7, Hampshire
Winchester, Chilcomb House, Vol. 7,
    Hampshire
Windsor, Cumberland Lodge, Vol. 10,
    Berkshire
Winestead, Vol. 3, Yorkshire
Wingerworth, Vol. 8, Derbyshire
Winslow, Vol. 4, Buckinghamshire
Winterborne Bassett, Vol. 4, Wiltshire
Winterbourne, Vol. 4, Berkshire
Wirksworth, Vol. 8, Derbyshire
Wishaw, Vol. 1, Warwickshire
Wissington, Vol. 2, Suffolk
Wistow, Vol. 8, Leicestershire
Withersfield, Vol. 2, Suffolk
Witherslack, Vol. 3, Westmorland
Withyham, Vol. 5, Sussex
Wittenham, Long, Vol. 4, Berkshire
Witton, East, Vol. 10, Yorkshire
Woburn Abbey, Vol. 4, Bedfordshire
Wolford Chapel, Vol. 7, Devon
Wolford Manor, Little, Vol. 1, Warwick-
    shire
Wollaston, Vol. 1, Northamptonshire
Wolston, Vol. 1, Warwickshire
Wolverley, Vol. 1, Worcestershire
Wonawtow, Vol. 9, Monmouthshire
Wonersh, Vol. 5, Surrey
Wooburn, Vol. 4, Buckinghamshire
Wood Eaton, Vol. 4, Oxfordshire
Woodbridge, Vols. 2 & 10, Suffolk

Woodbury, Vol. 7, Devon
Woodrising, Vol. 2, Norfolk
Woodton, Vol. 2, Norfolk
Woolley, Vol. 7, Somerset
Woolley, Vol. 3, Yorkshire
Woolwich, St Mary, Vol. 5, Kent
Wootton, Vol. 4, Bedfordshire
Wootton St Lawrence, Vol. 7, Hampshire
Wootton Wawen, Vol. 1, Warwickshire
Worcester, City Museum, Vol. 10,
    Worcestershire
Worfield, Vol. 9, Shropshire
Wormbridge, Vol. 9, Herefordshire
Wormhill, Vol. 8, Derbyshire
Wormington, Vol. 7, Gloucestershire
Worstead, Vol. 2, Norfolk
Wortham, Vol. 2, Suffolk
Worthenbury, Vol. 9, Wales
Wortley, Vol. 3, Yorkshire
Wragby, Nostell Priory, Vols. 3 & 10,
    Yorkshire
Wrenbury, Vol. 8, Cheshire
Wrentham, Vol. 2, Suffolk
Wrexham, Plas Power, Vol. 9, Wales
Writtle, Vol. 6, Essex
Wrockwardine, Vol. 9, Shropshire
Wroxall, Vol. 1, Warwickshire
Wroxeter, Vol. 9, Shropshire
Wycliffe, Vol. 3, Yorkshire
Wycombe Abbey, Vol. 4, Buckinghamshire
Wycombe, West, Vol. 4, Buckinghamshire
Wye, Vol. 5, Kent
Wymondham, Vol. 2, Norfolk

Yarcombe, Vol. 7, Devon
Yardley, Vols. 1 & 10, Warwickshire
Yardley Hastings, Vol. 1, Northamptonshire
Yarmouth, Vol. 7, Isle of Wight
Yarmouth, Great, St Nicholas, Vol. 2,
    Norfolk
Yaxley, Vol. 2, Suffolk
Yeovil, Vol. 7, Somerset
York, Holy Trinity, Micklegate, Vol. 3,
    Yorkshire
York, St Crux Hall, Vol. 3, Yorkshire
York, St Cuthbert, Vol. 3, Yorkshire
York, St William's College, Vols. 3 & 10,
    Yorkshire
Yoxford, Vol. 2, Suffolk

BIBLIOGRAPHY

Bayley, T. D. S. and Steer, F. W., 'Painted Heraldic Panels', *Antiquaries Journal*, Vol. 35 (1955), 68-87.

Burnett, C. J., *Funeral Heraldry in Scotland* (with particular reference to Hatchments). (Society of Antiquaries of Scotland, 1986).

Egerton, Sir P. (ed.), *The Life of William, Lord Grey of Wilton*, K.G. (Camden Society, Vol. 40, 1847).

Ellis, L. B., *Royal Hatchments in City Churches*. (London and Middlesex Arch. Soc. Transactions, New Series, Vol. 10, 1948), 24-30.

Gillings, C., *Death, Burial and the Individual in Early Modern England* (London, 1984).

Kemp, B., *English Church Monuments* (Batsford 1980).

Litten, J., *The English Way of Death* (1991).

Llewellyn, N., *The Art of Death* (1991).

Markham, C. A., *Hatchments, Northampton & Oakham* (Architectural Soc. Proceedings, Vol. 20, Pt 2 1912), 673-687.

Nichols, J. G., *The Diary of Henry Machyn* (Camden Society, Vol. 42, 1848).

Raines, F. R. (ed.), *Letters on the claims of the College of Arms in Lancashire in the time of James I* (Vol. 96, 1875).

INDEX